W9-BWQ-713

GIFT OF
JIM BECKER
© DEMCO, INC.—Archive Safe

Radical Political Economy

Radical Political Economy

An Introduction to the Alternative Economics

Brian Burkitt

New York University Press
New York *and* London
1984

First published in the U.S.A. in 1984 by
New York University Press,
Washington Square,
New York, N.Y. 10003

Library of Congress Cataloging in Publication Data

Burkitt, Brian.
Radical political economy.

Bibliography: p.
1. Marxian economics. 2. Socialism. I. Title.
HB97.5.B873 1984 335 84-2124
ISBN 0-8147-1057-3
ISBN 0-8147-1058-1 (pbk.)

Typeset in 11/12 point Times by
Alacrity Phototypesetters,
Banwell Castle, Weston-super-Mare
Printed and bound in Great Britain by
Butler & Tanner Ltd,
Frome, Somerset

To TIGER

the Conservative who
slept on all my manuscripts

Contents

Acknowledgements

This book attempts to assemble the salient features of those radical economic theories that have developed as an alternative to orthodox economics. While teaching a Radical Political Economy course at the University of Bradford, I became aware that no book surveying the different varieties of radical doctrine is available for undergraduates with no previous knowledge of this area. I hope that the present volume may help to fill the gap. It could not have been written without the active support of my colleagues and the critical contributions of my students. I am grateful to them all.

Specific thanks are due to John Dunworth, Ralph Herdan, Michael Surr, Margaret Wilkinson and Peter Wilson for discussing many of the issues raised here, to Peter Ketley for assiduously uncovering obscure references and to Kathleen Temple for converting my illegible drafts into a neat and error-free typescript. Brenda and Rachel provided a stimulating domestic environment and I am indebted to Rachel for the radical view of a younger generation. Nigel Copperthwaite was extremely supportive in a professional context and his toleration of my 'absences due to writing' has been beyond the call of friendship. Others have been equally tolerant, particularly Dorothy Clifton who insists that economics should and can be made intelligible to non-specialists. All those mentioned above, and many others, are responsible for whatever virtues this book may possess, but the source for errors and omissions lies within me.

Brian Burkitt,
Guiseley, September, 1983

1 Introduction

Radical political economists[1] unite in their distaste for capitalism and their preference for socialism, a fundamental outlook that provides the metaphysical base for their economic theories. There are, however, many possible definitions of socialism. Perhaps Dickinson (1939) provides most common ground: 'socialism is an economic organisation of society in which the material means of production are owned by the whole community and operated by organs representative of and responsible to a general economic plan, all members of the community being entitled to benefit from the results of such socialised planned production on the basis of equal rights'. Socialism is a multi-dimensional concept embracing simultaneously at least three facets; it is a system of abstract ideas and theories, it is a political movement seeking to achieve a programme of social transformation, and since 1917 it has been a structure of actual institutions under which certain countries function. A variety of socialisms are possible in each dimension, as are the possible verdicts upon their performance. Classification therefore gives rise to severe problems.

Radicals and their opponents alike agree that socialism rests upon a concern for 'equality'. Ultimately, advocacy of equality is a value judgement that people are born equal, in the sense that their equal humanity is more important than their different endowments. Socialists value equality not on the pragmatic grounds of its economic effects (for example, the Keynesian concern over deficient aggregate demand) but for its own sake because they:

(i) agree with Rainborough, the Civil War Leveller, that 'the poorest he that is in England hath a life to live as the greatest he',

(ii) believe that, while no distribution exactly equates reward with service, a nearly equal one is more likely to do so than a less equal one,

(iii) are convinced that the more evenly wealth is divided, the more welfare it promotes.

Radicals vary on the degree of equality they seek, but all desire that degree which they believe will establish the economic framework of a classless society, *i.e.* one where people are not separated from each other by variations in wealth and origin. They attempt to prove that capitalism is inherently exploitative and to develop models of the transition from the existing economic structure to socialism.

Capitalism is distinguished by the private ownership of non-human productive resources by either individuals or institutions, who are obliged to make a profit if they want to stay in business and must therefore place financial calculation foremost among their concerns. Because private ownership entails property rights, transition to socialism can never be simply a technical matter but involves a shift of power based upon a qualitative change in social relationships aimed at achieving human fraternity.

THE ESSENTIAL INGREDIENTS OF A THEORY OF CAPITALIST EXPLOITATION

All schools of economic thought develop a model of general equilibrium under specified conditions in order to unravel the tendencies and outcome of a system. In a capitalist market every commodity has its price, and incomes are derived from the sale of productive resources. Consequently radicals endeavour to construct a theory of long-run equilibrium prices where:

(i) capital represents a coercive social power acting through a market structure (competitive or otherwise),

(ii) workers are exploited by capitalists, who appropriate the product of their labour in the form of profit, rent and interest.

A comprehensive and consistent theory of capitalist exploitation is an essential element of radical political economy. It requires four ingredients:

(i) a set of propositions defining exploitation, which contain (a) verifiable descriptive statements about the structure of the economy and its institutional framework, and (b) statements of what 'ought to be' or 'could be' in contrast to the status quo,

(ii) the incorporation of exp;oitation as defined in (i) into a theory of long-run equilibrium prices under capitalism, complete with proofs of the existence and uniqueness of equilibrium. Exploitation is an inadequate explanation of profits and property incomes in a market economy unless product prices are determined in a way that is consistent with its existence,

(iii) a statement of why exploitation inevitably remains positive at long-run equilibrium,

(iv) a set of empirically verifiable predictions about the tendencies of capitalist evolution and why they are unlikely to eliminate exploitation within an economy based on private ownership of the non-human productive resources.

Radicals see exploitation as ineradicably engrained in capitalism so that their models rest upon the inevitable logic of the system. Belief that exploitation constitutes an inherent element of capitalist-worker relations is distinct from less analytical observations that labour often receives low pay or that many live in poverty while others enjoy wealth. These observations may create a favourable atmosphere for the reception of exploitation theories, but to accept the latter it is essential that the wage contract *implies* exploitation; it is insufficient that such contracts are frequently associated with exploitation or an inadequate standard of living. A comprehensive theory does not rest simply on metaphysical statements or ethical value judgements but describes the characteristics of the social structure from which relative prices and income distribution emerge.

Exploitation reflects and generates differences in power and advantage[2] which have additional dimensions to the financial one. Differential power and advantage create individual and class variations across the whole range of life chances, which become generalised and establish future inequalities of opportunity. They prove resistant to change because the privileged possess both the motivation and the resources to maintain their position and transmit it to their offspring. Consequently the abolition of exploitation is unlikely to result as a by-product of such developments as technical change or economic growth but will require conscious collective action.

UTOPIAN CRITIQUES OF POLITICAL ECONOMY

Although elements of radical analysis and inspirations tending towards socialism can be traced back to Greek philosophy and Judean-Christian traditions, theories asserting the inevitability of capitalist exploitation developed largely in response to eighteenth-century industrialisation and the associated elaboration of political economy as an independent discipline. Radical models arose from criticism of both capitalist economies and of the doctrines that justified conditions within them. In eighteenth-century Britain economic liberalism and the separation of wage labour from capital began to operate over most of society, and many economists expounded the benefits to be derived from these phenomena. In response concepts of cooperation, *i.e.* collective activity that excludes individual competition and the pursuit of profit, and proposals for socialising the means of production evolved as methods to overcome exploitation.

Marx labelled his radical predecessors as 'Utopians', a term derived from the title of a book written by Sir Thomas More around 1516. However, the usage of this word requires careful consideration; it does not imply that Utopian doctrines were inherently impractical but that they were unimplementable at the time they were advanced. Utopians made no attempt to outline any strategy of transition towards their objectives, while they failed to establish contact with an existing or potential source of power that could act as an agent of economic and social transformation. Their ideas could only be implemented with bourgeois aid (usually envisaged as operating through state institutions) or through a moral revolution, since no force was indicated as moving toward the goal. Consequently supporters of Utopian arguments had no practical course of action available to them.

However, Utopian ideas were not uninfluential because:

(i) they were not simply dreams of individuals but rationalised certain aspirations held by the non-ruling classes,

(ii) they provided useful concepts and tools of analysis for later radicals, including the very idea of socialism itself,

(iii) some Utopians enjoyed contact with mass movements, for example the Levellers in the English Civil War and Babeuf during the French Revolution. However, this involvement was sporadic and did not spring from fundamental principle, so that it differed in kind from the Marxist identification of the working class as the source of socialist power.

It was Marx who averred, and sought to establish, the existence of a trend towards socialism and the necessity of permanent contact with a potential power base. These are two necessary conditions for socialism to become a major political force. There was, however, no continuous tradition of radical economics in Britain before the nineteenth century, although earlier isolated critiques of social conditions provided the foundation from which later ideas emerged. In particular, they pointed to the extraction of unpaid labour by the possessing class. Because workers do not own the instruments of production with which they work, they are compelled, after selling their labour power, to work longer than is necessary to support themselves. The revenue from these extra hours of production accrues to the capitalist. Such contributions to radical political economy remained largely intuitive until the industrial revolution stimulated socialist thought, and seem remote today, but they bequeathed the notion that private property was the source of existing inequality and exploitation. In subsequent chapters I trace the development of radical economic theory in an approximately chronological order, concentrating upon the two periods when it developed rapidly — the half-century before the First World War and the last twenty years. I focus almost entirely on radical thought within advanced industrial economies and neglect the very different issues raised in developing countries.

SYNOPSIS OF THE SUCCEEDING CHAPTERS

Modern radical economics is largely a response to the problems posed, first in Britain and then in a successively greater number of countries, by industrialisation. Chapter Two assesses the costs incurred by workers during the eighteenth- and early nineteenth-century industrial revolution and traces the career of Robert Owen, one of the first radical thinkers to respond to the new situation.

Contemporary with Owen were a group of economists who used the theories developed by Ricardo in an attempt to construct the first comprehensive model of capitalist exploitation. This group became known as the Ricardian Socialists and their contribution is outlined in Chapter Three.

Karl Marx made overwhelmingly the most significant radical contribution, whether measured in terms of analytical range or of subsequent political influence. Chapters Four and Five discuss, in so far as they can be distinguished, the specifically economic elements of Marx's synthesis.

Marxist socialism soon became the principal anti-capitalist

philosophy in a number of industrialising countries, notably Germany and Austria, but towards the end of the nineteenth century alternative forms of socialism based on detailed economic analyses emerged. In Britain the Fabians rejected the labour theory of value and substituted their own model of capitalist exploitation. Fabian economics is the subject of Chapter Six.

In France, Spain and the United States the socio-economic environment was not conducive to the emergence of a mass political movement based on either Marxism or Fabianism. Greater emphasis was accordingly placed upon the potential industrial power of trade unions. Chapter Seven discusses the doctrine of Syndicalism which justified this emphasis, and also considers its British variant, Guild Socialism.

Since the 1870s the neoclassical paradigm, which analyses how marginal market adjustments produce an equilibrium structure of relative prices, has been the accepted framework for approaching economic problems among almost all non-Marxists. By concentrating upon individual adaptations within a given socio-economic environment rather than the determinants of that environment, neoclassical economists tend to support, implicitly or explicitly, the status quo in a market economy. Indeed when pursued to its logical conclusion, *e.g.* by Friedman (1972), this paradigm constitutes one of the strongest positive justifications for a capitalist economic system. However, theories of exploitation under capitalism can be developed from a neoclassical perspective and these are outlined in Chapter Eight.

Chapter Nine discusses the theory of transition from capitalism to socialism advanced by Schumpeter. This theory is unique, partly because Schumpeter was an opponent of socialism, but mainly because it rests on the premise that capitalism will be undermined not by its failure but by its success.

In recent years radical political economy, despite its lack of immediate political success, has been expanding rapidly to the point where there are now more trained radical economists developing their own form of scholarship than at any other time. Chapter Ten traces the themes that marked this re-emergence, focussing particularly upon the Capital Controversy, analysis of reswitching and capital reversing, and the construction of non-marginal theories of distribution.

Chapter Eleven concludes that, although radicals face considerable problems in achieving theoretical unity among themselves and in extending their wider influence, there are concrete reasons for radical optimism. One prediction that can be made confidently is that the economic theories discussed in this book, and the ideologies underlying them, will be the subject of further development and controversy in the future.

NOTES

1 In this book radical economists are classified as those seeking greater equality through communal ownership. We exclude those wishing to restore a more individualistic version of capitalism, many of whom see themselves as 'radical'.

2 Power can be defined as the capacity to mobilise resources, human and non-human, to achieve a desired state of affairs, while advantage can be defined as the possession of, and control over, whatever is valued. The two attributes are closely related; power is used to secure advantage, while advantage constitutes some of the resources used in exercising power.

2 Robert Owen

The industrial revolution that gathered momentum in Britain during the late eighteenth century stimulated radical political economy. Utopians argued that private property was the source of existing inequalities but the framework of their thought, based upon conceptions of a pre-industrial society, is today remote. The extensive development of factory production, the social conditions that ensued and the interpretation of these events favoured by conventional economists created the conditions in which modern socialism was born.

THE SOCIAL COSTS OF THE INDUSTRIAL REVOLUTION

The industrial revolution brought about unprecendented increases in productivity based on the development of factories and the widespread use of machinery. The major cost of these innovations was borne by those with least power. In 1750 the working class lived near subsistence level and the purchasing power of wages deteriorated during the second half of the eighteenth century, while the controversy among economic historians[1] as to whether real wages rose between 1800 and 1850 suggests that any improvement was only slight. However, national income grew over this period, so that workers' relative living standards fell and the potential consumption they involuntarily sacrificed financed the investment required for industrialisation. Had working-class incomes kept in step with national income, the average worker would have been approximately fifty per cent richer in 1840 than thirty years earlier.[2] No historian claims that this occurred.

Qualitative deteriorations in the environment reinforced quantitative trends. Workers lost access to ownership of the means of production, and therefore the possibility of independence, as fewer could bear the cost of the equipment now necessary for efficiency. The capital required to put technical knowledge into effect grew more expensive, until its acquisition came to be beyond the financial capacity of most people, whose sole means of livelihood was to offer themselves for employment as machine operators. Specialised, monotonous factory routine replaced traditional jobs, while to reap full economies of scale capitalists subjected workers to a structure of discipline which maximised the effort supplied. Mechanisation facilitated the division of labour, creating tasks that women and children could perform. Consequently whole families often worked to achieve subsistence. The conditions under which labour was performed were unregulated,[3] dangerous and involved long hours.

The growth of factory production stimulated urbanisation; in 1750 only two British cities had a population greater than 50,000, but a hundred years later the total was twenty-nine. Street cleansing, water supply and the provision of open spaces failed to keep pace with urban migration, while housing was concentrated in crowded slums. The inevitable result was air and water pollution, epidemics of typhoid and cholera, and widespread respiratory and intestinal disease, with a consequent low expectation of life. In addition to being driven from the land by enclosures, made redundant or exposed to the competition of child labour by new machines and enwalled in factory towns, workers suffered the additional burden of political persecution due to government fears of a repetition of the French Revolution. Successive administrations were slow to remedy social problems, intervened to maintain the price of bread and impeded the development of trade unions.

Today Cole's (1952) verdict is widely accepted, *i.e.* the period of the Napoleonic War and the subsequent economic crisis constituted the blackest chapter in British labour history, when the foundations of modern industry were erected on the suffering of workers denied access to the fruits of an expanding economy. By contrast, capitalists enjoyed absolute power over their labour force, in pursuit of expanding profits. The industrial revolution created the modern working class, nominally free but able to live only by selling labour power. Britain witnessed in response a considerable development of radical economic doctrines in the first half of the nineteenth century.

THE RADICAL REACTION TO INDUSTRIALISATION

Late eighteenth- and early nineteenth-century industrialisation rested on three sets of institutional data — private property in the means of production, a self-regulating market economy and the transformation of labour into a commodity. Orthodox economists either took as given or positively approved these phenomena but many Conservatives and socialists opposed them. Such 'Tory Radicals' as Oastler and Shaftesbury maintained a paternalist ethic based either on Christianity or an aristocratic disdain for industry. These views seemed impractical in ignoring the productive potential of industry and assuming that earlier life styles remained viable.

Radicals, however, accepted industrial techniques but not the unrestrained rule of private capital or a self-regulating market, which they argued were the ultimate causes of contemporary inequalities and social problems. They believed that, through elimination of the private ownership of capital, an industrial economy would be created where every person was treated with dignity and the proceeds of production were divided equitably. The operation of the economy was then criticised by reference to such an ideal. Perhaps the most influential early nineteenth-century British socialist was Robert Owen.

OWEN AS INDUSTRIALIST AND ECONOMIST

Owen (1771-1858) achieved fame as a businessman, an economic theorist and a social reformer. From the age of ten he served as a draper's apprentice but at twenty he was the manager of a large cotton factory at New Lanark, which became renowned throughout Britain for its conditions of work. Owen was a benevolent autocrat who insisted on strict industrial discipline, but in combination with living wages, a decent job environment and compulsory education for workers' children. He strove to maximise profits and believed that the profitability of New Lanark demonstrated the shortsightedness of other capitalists' treatment of their workers. Despite the admiration he received as a successful businessman, he was regarded as eccentric because of his condemnation of a social order based on private enterprise and his anti-religious sentiments.

Owen's industrial management rested on his belief that environmental improvements were the means to progress. His central tenet, that human character is moulded by circumstances, places policy emphasis upon alterations in the environment with education the key. He saw human nature as malleable, with society being the formative influence. On this basis, Owen wrought decisive changes at New Lanark. He created infant schools as a substitute for child labour, enforced standards of cleanliness and abolished public houses. These reforms were easier to implement because he wielded the unrestrained authority of capital in his factory and in the town. Over the years Owen gradually attempted to extend his influence. He saw his successful experiment at New Lanark as a precursor for national policies, *i.e.* an improvement of the overall environment by legislation to inculcate rationalism, the abolition of child labour, drinking, gambling and the punishment of crime, plus the collection of statistics on the condition of labour by a state which assumes responsibility for providing work for the unemployed.

These proposals emanated from Owen's distinctive economic philosophy. Although many of its components remained underdeveloped, its essential elements were these:

(i) The experience of New Lanark convinced Owen of the validity of what later was termed the 'Economy of High Wages', which holds that a wage increase may produce an increase in labour's productivity due to a direct improvement in workers' efficiency arising out of their improved living standards or to greater efficiency in use of the other factors of production in response to higher labour costs. In such circumstances, rises in wages generate additional revenue from which they can be paid. Owen's theory conflicted with the prevailing orthodoxy which stated that any wage increase occurred at the expense of profits and hence led to a diminution in employment and economic activity.

(ii) Owen saw an individualistic economy as inequitable, irrational and anti-social, arguing that private ownership was an institution whereby one class gained power over the rest in order to gain profits. In contrast he stressed that the greatest collective benefit accrued only when people cooperated to control nature. He did not attack industry or new technology, but denounced private ownership of the means of production, the unrestrained spread of competition and the notion that people could better themselves by individual effort.

(iii) Owen held a rudimentary labour theory of value which he attempted to apply on behalf of the working class. He saw human labour as 'the natural standard of value' and thought that this concept required machinery to become the servant of labour. He wanted the state to determine the amount of labour expended on commodities and then ensure that they are exchanged on this basis.

(iv) By extending the 'Economy of High Wages' from an individual firm to the nation, Owen embraced an embryonic underconsumption theory of depressions. He advocated a high wage policy that maintained purchasing power as a cure for unemployment.

(v) Owen opposed the Malthusian theory of population. He believed that New Lanark illustrated the possibility of expanding output and real wages simultaneously while environmental reforms and the establishment of new social relations prevent a rise in the birth rate when real wages increase.

(vi) Owen's solution to contemporary problems focussed upon cooperation as the motive economic force, operating through a network of self-governing communes, where private ownership of the means of production is abolished and the quest for profit eliminated. He visualised a brotherhood of equals that would be impossible to attain if owners of capital deployed machinery in their own interests or if each employer was driven by competition to force down the price of labour. The solution of present difficulties and the future blueprint lay in the conscious organisation of production by self-governing communities.

OWEN'S CAREER AS A SOCIAL REFORMER

Owen's career as a national reformer fell into distinct stages. Between the publication of *Towards a New View of Society* in 1813 and *A Report to the County of Lanark* in 1821, he concentrated upon ameliorating existing social problems such as poverty, child labour, long hours and unemployment. He thought that these could be avoided if his fellow manufacturers copied New Lanark on grounds of enlightened self-interest. Indeed his arguments at this stage could be shared by capitalists more concerned with long-term profitability than with immediate gains, but he found that his appeals met with little response. He then attempted to persuade the government to alleviate social distress. He was intermitently popular in official circles after 1815 when he stressed the importance of environmental improvements more than socialism. As he advanced beyond the role of wealthy philanthropist to the advocacy of wider reforms that threatened established authority, he became less influential.

Failure led Owen into attempts at achieving reform by examples that would demonstrate its benefits. Thus he established communist communities at Orbiston (near Glasgow), Tytherley (in Hampshire) and between 1824 and 1829 at New Harmony in Indiana. Their aim was to settle unemployed labourers on the land in self-governed 'Villages of Unity and Cooperation'. Such schemes reflected his conviction that society as then constituted would permit cooperatives to supplant existing institutional structures. At this stage of his career as social reformer Owen was still preaching to the rich and influential. All the Owenite settlements declined and ultimately disappeared, partly because of internal administrative difficulties, partly because of the hostile external environment and partly because of the agricultural depression which generated an influx of unemployed workers, and thus excess supply of labour, to the villages of cooperation. The establishment and collapse of these schemes devoured a large proportion of Owen's wealth.

In 1824 the London Cooperative Society was formed as a store for cooperative trading, designed to supersede competitive distribution and allow craftsmen to exchange goods without capitalist intermediaries. It aimed to sell at trade prices and use the savings accumulated through elimination of retailers' profits to establish socialist communities. The next envisaged stage of development involved members' cooperation to produce directly for each other rather than choosing between capitalist goods sold in their stores; in 1830 the London Society opened an Exchange Bazaar for societies and individuals to engage in mutual exchange. Owen returned from the United States in 1829, when more than three hundred cooperative societies were in existence, a figure which rose to almost five hundred by 1832, although many pursued solely educational objectives. After 1830 producers' societies aiming to supply cooperative stores developed rapidly. They arose first in trades requiring little capital, and were particularly attractive to craftsmen whose independent status was threatened by capitalist production methods. They often possessed close connections with the relevant trade unions, which saw them as auxiliaries in the struggle for better conditions by providing jobs for the unemployed and those on strike. In 1831 the first National Cooperative Congress met, at which Owen fostered producers' cooperatives as a means of converting even more unions to the creed of cooperation.

Cooperative stores bought wholesale, and sold retail, the commodities demanded by their members, but cooperative producers faced the difficult problem of obtaining a market for all their products. This problem stimulated development of labour exchanges, where workmen and producers' cooperatives could exchange products directly, so dispensing with both employers and merchants. The most important such institution, the National Equitable Labour Exchange, was set up by Owen in 1832 and stimulated the formation of similar exchanges in provincial cities. They sought to secure a wider market for cooperative groups and to enable them to exchange their products at an equitable valuation resting on labour time. Owen appointed trade union valuers to price goods on the basis of the cost of raw materials plus the amount of labour time expended on them. A new currency of labour notes was issued for the conduct of transactions.

Exchanges obtained a brisk supply of goods most of which were bought readily, while in an era of small banks' note issue labour notes were initially accepted outside the cooperative movement. However, crucial weaknesses emerged. Labour and commercial prices coexisted uneasily; goods the exchanges offered more cheaply were soon disposed of but the more expensive remained unsold. Exchanges would not control their stocks to demand levels and movements in the manner of capitalist retailers, since they had to take what members brought to them. Consequently they became overstocked where there were many cooperative producers and understocked in trades where there were few. In practice their supplies were concentrated upon goods that could be produced by craftsmen possessing little capital. Despite this major weakness, they enjoyed considerable success for a time, but collapsed in the general crash of the movement in 1834. Even then some exchanges balanced their books, but the National Equitable Labour Exchange incurred a heavy debt which fell on Owen.

When Owen returned to England in 1829, he found that a trade union movement had emerged after the repeal of the Combination Acts in 1824. 1829 witnessed the formation of the first modern national union, the Operative Spinners, while the following two years saw much social unrest in the form of agricultural riots and a wave of strike activity in the northern textile towns as a means of achieving the eight-hour day. Therefore by 1832 several distinct but related bodies, such as Owenite societies, cooperative stores, cooperative producers, labour exchanges and trade unions, looked to Owen for leadership. Most were growing rapidly, as workers disillusioned by the terms of the 1832 Reform Act, swung away from political, towards industrial, action. Owen sought the fusion of these groups into one national organisation, centrally directed and under socialist control, that would endeavour to overthrow capitalism and transform economic relations through its practice of cooperative production.

By 1833 the Operative Builders' Union was the largest in the country, with a membership of sixty thousand. It adopted an Owenite programme to take over the construction industry and reorganise it as a national guild. To implement this programme, none of its members would work for capitalist builders who refused to join the guild, which would be the sole employer, administered by elected managers and paying its members whether in or out of work. The capitalists attempted to destroy the O.B.U. by a lockout; they re-employed only those workers who signed the document (*i.e.* a written pledge not to join a union, which gives an employer the right to sack them if they violate it). The workers lost as the O.B.U. simultaneously fought the lockout and attempted to launch the guild with inadequate financial resources. Its members were forced back to capitalists' employment region by region during 1834 and by the end of that year the O.B.U. ceased to exist. It split into craft sections with a greatly reduced membership.

Owen sought to unite 'all the associations intended for the improvement of the working classes'. To this end he inspired the formation of the Grand National Consolidated Trades Union which was intended to be a single inclusive union aiming to supersede capitalism by a cooperative system based upon workers' control of production. It sought to implement on an economy-wide basis a plan similar to the O.B.U. guild for construction. Ultimately the G.N.C.T.U. would control, through its constituent members, all industry, thereby taking over the functions of capitalists, parliament and local government. It would become the locus of economic, and ultimately political, power. The G.N.C.T.U.'s formation was followed by feverish organisation; discounting cooperative retail and producer societies, unions alone attracted over one million members (the figure does not include the membership of two large unions, the Operative Builders and the Yorkshire Trades Union organising in wool textiles, which chose to stay outside the G.N.C.T.U.).

As with the O.B.U., capitalists reacted to the G.N.C.T.U. by presenting the document to workers, with the threat of a lockout if not signed. This response originated in Derby; it was imitated in other towns but Derby remained the test-struggle. The workers lost, being forced back to work after a lockout lasting four months. This severe setback to the G.N.C.T.U. was followed by the notorious 'Tolpuddle Martyrs' court decision, under which unionists were transported for administering unlawful oaths. Given the repeal of the Combination Acts, the case was pursued under the 1797 Naval Mutinies Act which was never intended to apply to trade unions. This opportunity for the government to deter union organisation arose because many unions adopted secret initiation ceremonies under the threat of employer retaliation.

The G.N.C.T.U. encountered severe administrative problems. The recruits it made and the disputes it faced were so many that urgent problems of management were inevitably ignored. Internal dissension developed and Owen became disillusioned; he hoped to initiate bloodless revolution by providing examples of the benefits derived from cooperation, not to become a leader of mass industrial disputes. Accordingly he dissolved the G.N.C.T.U. in August 1834, arguing for a return to education and the need for an ethical appeal in preference to coercion. The G.N.C.T.U. faded away, but some of its constituent groups and elements of its cooperative ideology remained. Owen returned to establishing villages of cooperation (*e.g.* Queenswood in 1839), and in 1844 the Rochdale Pioneers' Cooperative Society, forerunner of the modern movement, developed from a local Owenite body. However, after 1834 the thrust of working-class agitation moved from industrial to political arenas, focussing upon the demands of the Chartists.

The G.N.C.T.U. was undoubtedly a failure. It suffered from weak, incompetent leadership, inadequate thought and lack of finance, yet it was attempting an impossible task which no leadership could have achieved; trade unions were still learning the art of combination (they had enjoyed less than ten years to organise), capitalism had not fully developed its productive potential and the working class was immature. Workers could accomplish sporadic revolt but not yet sustained action. By contrast, capitalists were strong and determined, having just won a great political victory in the 1832 Reform Act. They also possessed the support of a Whig government determined to show that the Reform Act would not destroy property rights. Against such power, workers were poorly paid, uneducated and only beginning to organise. Owen's career as a social reformer must be assessed in terms of this hostile environment.

CONCLUSION: OWEN'S INFLUENCE

Although Owen's schemes beyond the sphere of New Lanark failed during his lifetime, he bequeathed an enduring legacy to future radicals:

(i) The personal example of one who cast aside wealth in an endeavour to secure a happier future for others.

(ii) The paternalistic measures at New Lanark illustrated that a policy of high wages and improved conditions need not destroy profitability. Owen thus initiated a new attitude to wage questions, as demonstrated by the emergence of a labour aristocracy in the 1850s, and he became unwittingly the forerunner of the modern 'soulful corporation'.

(iii) Many of Owen's theoretical innovations (*e.g.* labour values to replace money; an Equitable Labour Exchange) are not inherently impractical, the degree of their success depending upon institutional circumstances.

(iv) His theories of, and attempts to establish, workers' cooperatives made Owen the instigator of a significant movement of later times, as developments from the Rochdale Pioneers of 1844 demonstrate.

(v) Owen's appreciation of the role of trade unions in replacing individual worker motivations by collective policy provided a clue to improving quantitative and qualitative living standards, and also pointed to a force that could potentially be harnessed for achieving a future transformation of productive relations.

(vi) Owen's career epitomised the Utopian approach and dilemma. He hoped first for individual conversion, then government action and then the illustrative effect of example. Personal behaviour, political reform and 'trail blazing' were seen as potentially transforming because an agent initiated voluntary changes, but he identified no social force capable of working towards his goal, so that capitalist or state aid was required to achieve it. This was an unrealisable ambition given the existing power structure. Owen lacked a theory of class struggle, believing instead that transition to socialism would occur through the influence of reason, practically demonstrated. Owen's career was a social reformer was a failure, but he bequeathed an important legacy, and, despite his lack of success as a leader, no personal qualities could in the 1830s have converted the G.N.C.T.U. into a vehicle for achieving his ideals.

NOTES

1 Taylor (1960) summarised the major contributions to this controversy.
2 This calculation is based on the national income estimates of Deane (1956).
3 The first effective Factory Act was not implemented until 1833.

3 The Ricardian Socialists

The advent of factory production stimulated the development of political economy and soon a gulf emerged between the approach of conventional economists and that of radicals. Orthodoxy held that private ownership of the means of production would ultimately prove beneficial to all, while socialists maintained that any system treating labour as a commodity was inherently immoral. Under capitalism, they argued, labour was subordinated to the unregulated process whereby capital reproduced itself, simultaneously recreating workers' servile condition. Far from being recognised as the most basic human activity on which industry was founded, labour became a necessity into which free people were forced by financial circumstances. Its emancipation required the abolition of capitalism and its replacement by collective ownership. Chapter Two considered the attempts made to put these ideals into practice under the leadership of Robert Owen. Simultaneously a group of radical economists constructed the first comprehensive theory of capitalist exploitation. The group is known today as the Ricardian Socialists.

THE BASIC PROPOSITIONS OF RICARDIAN SOCIALIST THEORY

If all radicals influenced by the ideas of Ricardo are defined as 'Ricardian Socialists', Marx would be included, but the term is used more narrowly to describe those economists who in the 1820s and 1830s developed a theory of capitalist exploitation from the proposition that labour is the only source of wealth. The most prominent were Ravenstone, Thompson, Gray, Hodgskin and Bray. Although they differed in detail, they all argued that labour is the sole factor of production and that exploitation is an inevitable component of employer-worker relations in an economy based upon private ownership. Although the first proposition has a long history extending at least to Locke, Ricardo's version of the labour theory of value provided new stimulus to radical political economy.

Exploitation theories rationalise workers' resentment at the rich living off the proceeds of manual labour, but the Ricardian Socialists went further by arguing that capitalism *necessarily* involved exploitation. This idea was suggested by Adam Smith's (1776) proposition that rent and interest are deductions from an output that in its entirety should be considered the produce of labour and by Ricardo's (1817) view of employers' functions, *i.e.* capitalists furnish workers with tools, raw materials and means of subsistence and receive these 'advances' back with a profit that is part of workers' industry. It is a short step from this concept to an exploitation theory of capitalist income; Ricardo failed to take it as he simultaneously propounded three other theories of profit (abstinence, productivity and residual), but the Ricardian Socialists did.

Their belief that exploitation is inherent to capital-labour relations is distinct from less analytical observations that workers are frequently treated unfairly or that many live in poverty while others enjoy wealth. Such observations may create attitudes responsive to exploitation theories, but to accept the latter it is essential that the wage contract *implies* exploitation; it is insufficient that it should often be associated with a low standard of living for wage earners. The Ricardian Socialists reached their conclusion concerning the inevitability of capitalist exploitation from three fundamental propositions:

(i) Labour is the only source of wealth.

(ii) The values of all commodities can be represented in terms of the labour hours embodied in them.

(iii) Labour itself is a commodity under capitalism.

These lead to the conclusion that workers are robbed by the market mechanism of the difference between the labour value of their product and the labour value of the amount of work invested in that product. The difference consists of various types of property income, ultimately reducible to profit, and its size measures the degree of exploitation. The existence of such a difference is not due to cheating or robbery (although these may occur), but to the ineradicable logic of a capitalist economy.

RICARDO'S LABOUR THEORY OF VALUE

Because Ricardian Socialists justified the claim of labour to the whole product of industry as a deduction from the labour theory of value advanced by Ricardo (1817), the latter requires consideration. Despite heated controversy concerning the validity of the labour theory of value, none can doubt its economic and politic significance.

Classical political economy focussed upon growth and distribution. It rested upon the labour theory of value, *i.e.* the idea that in all societies labour is the active creator of wealth and that other productive resources are merely the means through which wealth is generated. The value of commodities represents the labour time spent on producing them. By arguing that labour rather than gold or land is the ultimate source of wealth, the theory directs attention to those forces enabling productivity to increase rapidly. Thus it was used by orthodox economists in the late eighteenth century to attack laws and policies favouring the interests of landed property, and to support the demands of industrialists whose ownership of capital (representing past, stored-up labour) gave them the power to direct the production process, the organisation of which is crucial since it provides the material basis of life. Every society is obliged to establish some mechanism for allocating its citizens' labour between different uses and for distributing the proceeds among them. The only possible measure of aggregate labour is time, the number of hours of average skill and intensity that the population can work, because measurement would be circular if labour's value depended upon the price it commands. Economic analysis therefore rests upon an understanding of how available labour time is used.

Smith and Ricardo both accepted that labour was the source of wealth and that the value of commodities was measured by the quantity of labour embodied in them. For Smith, 'labour' includes that of the capitalist and the service of his capital in addition to the manual work performed by hired employees. In Ricardo's formulation, 'labour' incorporates capital, the past output, as well as the present output, of the workforce. Each left unchallenged capitalists' claims to share in the product. Such interpretations followed the attempts of Aristotle, the majority of medieval schoolmen, Petty and Locke to justify private property; for instance, Locke argued that labour, defined as entrepreneurship, gave a title to property. Therefore the labour theory of value was originally applied to the labour of the proprietor, while wage work was not seen as the creator of value. Indeed for Locke the employee's share was only a subsistence wage.

The novel aspect of the Ricardian Socialist approach was to use the labour theory of value as the foundation for a theory of capitalist exploitation, by arguing that the labour which is the source of all value is that of the wage worker, while the capitalist claim to profit was repudiated. Their task was eased by the specific form of Ricardo's theory which made circulating capital (*i.e.* primarily wage labour) the sole creator of value. Therefore the Ricardian Socialists amended traditional interpretations, which they felt to be incompatible with an industrial system which transformed owners of capital into controllers of labour. Ricardo's writings are unclear on whether he regarded labour as the *source* or merely the *measure* of value. The Ricardian Socialists adopted the first position and then defined capital as past, stored-up labour. Thus they derived from the labour theory of value a definition of exploitation which underpinned Owen's moral critique of capitalism.

THE RICARDIAN SOCIALIST THEORY OF CAPITALIST EXPLOITATION

According to the Preface of Ricardo's *Principles*, discovery of the laws which regulate distributive shares is the 'principal problem in Political Economy'. Ricardo's theory was based on two separate concepts, the marginal and the surplus principle. The former explains the share of rent and the latter the division of the residue between wages and profits.

Their operation is demonstrated by Figure One, where OY measures quantities of corn (chosen as a measure of commodities in general), while OX represents the labour employed in production. At a given state of knowledge with given resources, the schedule P-Ap shows the product per unit of labour and the schedule P-Mp the marginal product of labour. These curves are distinct because of a declining average product due to the operation of diminishing returns. Output is uniquely

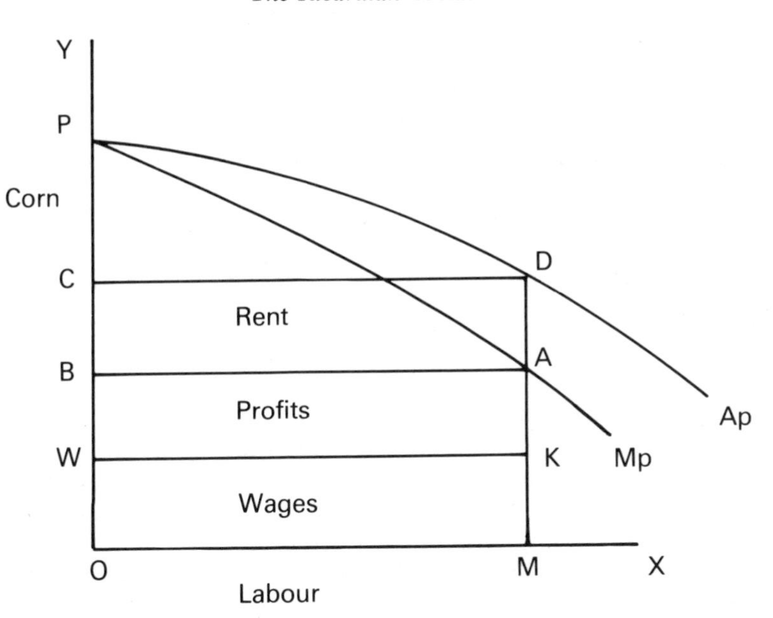

Figure One

determined when the quantity of labour is given[1]; with work-force OM, total output is represented by the rectangle OCDM. Rent is the difference between average and marginal labour productivity, which depends on the elasticity of the P-Ap schedule and thus on the speed at which diminishing returns operate.

The marginal product of labour is not equal to the wage, but to the sum of wages and profits. The rate of wages is determined independently of marginal productivity by the supply price of labour, assumed to be constant in terms of corn. Thus the Ricardian hypothesis implies an infinitely elastic supply of labour at the given supply price, OW. The basis of this assumption is the Malthusian theory of population, whereby numbers increase (indefinitely) when wages are above, and decrease (indefinitely) when they are below, the subsistence level. Ricardo's interpretation of the doctrine removed emphasis from a biologically determined subsistence supply price of labour, yet he retained the operative principle that in any given social environment there is a *natural* rate of wages, at which population remains constant and from which wages can deviate only temporarily.

For any given workforce, profits are residual arising from the difference between the marginal product of labour and the wage rate. The resulting ratio,

$$\frac{\text{profits}}{\text{wages}}$$

determines the rate of profit on the capital required. The Ricardian Socialists built upon this framework. Their main analytical innovations were as follows:

(i) They paid little attention to the law of diminishing returns and drew no theoretical distinction between rent and profits.

(ii) They did not subscribe to the Malthusian theory of population, so that they required another explanation for wages being tied to subsistence. They developed for this purpose a theory of exploitation based on the concept of 'unequal exchange' between capitalists and workers.

This theory derived from their interpretation of the labour theory of value, which defined labour as the only source of wealth and capital as the stored-up product of past labour which capitalists appropriate. Consequently capitalists make no contribution to production, while property incomes are a deduction from the product created by labour. Ravenstone (1821) summed up the Ricardian Socialist position in his pronouncement that 'the fund for the maintenance of the idle is the surplus produce of the labour of the industrious'. Hodgskin (1825) reiterated the supreme importance attached to labour as the sole factor of production; whoever may be the owner of fixed capital — and in the present state of society he who makes it and he who uses it is not — it is the hand and knowledge of the labourer which make it, preserve it from decay and use it to any beneficial end'. Land and capital are reduced to labour, without which neither can produce. Circulating capital becomes the co-existing labour of other workers (*e.g.* food eaten during production), while fixed capital is the product of past labour which is unproductive even when completed unless operated by people. Therefore the productivity of capital derives from labour, which should enjoy the right to the entire proceeds of industry.

This right was self-evidently not enjoyed in nineteenth-century Britain. If non-labour is unproductive and its income a tax upon those who produce, how does such appropriation arise? The Ricardian Socialists emphasised the institutional datum that under capitalism labourers do not own subsistence funds, which are advanced to them by capitalists. They accounted for the existence of property incomes by the empirical observation that most workers cannot wait for the proceeds of time-consuming production and urgently require means of livelihood during the intervening period. Given this inability to wait, the minority class that possesses the necessary funds can exact a price for their use. Here lies the source of capitalist profit, a dispossessed working class unable to wait to reap the fruits of its labour. The Ricardian Socialists argued that all property consists of no more than accumulated labour; capitalists depend both on the labour of others and on the historical and legal injustice that enables them to command it, despite the fact that inherited wealth derives from the social process of production. Their conclusion was that the fruits of accumulation should be regarded as a trust for future generations, over which individuals possess an equal claim.

The monopoly of the ability to wait enjoyed by capitalists means that exchanges in the labour market between those who own and those who do not own subsistence funds are inherently unequal. Inequality of exchange favours capitalists, so that profits are positive at long-run equilibrium and, given the definition of labour as the only source of wealth, the existence of profits implies that capitalists exploit workers. 'Profits', wrote Hodgskin (1825), 'are purely and simply a portion of the product of labour which the capitalist, without any right other than that conferred upon him by law, takes for himself'. Individual competition produces inequality due to the phenomenon of unequal exchange. Bray (1839) analysed this phenomenon in detail; because exchange is voluntary in a capitalist market, it usually involves mutual benefit but not necessarily, nor normally, equal benefit. Unequal exchange, where the capitalist returns only part of labour's product in return for its services, is the basic cause of exploitation. The remedy lies in replacing unequal with equal exchange, which can be achieved only by social changes to secure communality of possessions and the elimination of the capitalist class.

The Ricardian Socialists were the first economists to construct a comprehensive theory attempting to demonstrate the inevitability of exploitation at the competitive capitalist equilibrium. The right of labour, as the sole active creator of wealth, to total output is obstructed by the institutional apparatus of capitalism, which gives rise to unequal exchange and allows employers, who enjoy a monopoly of the ability to wait through ownership of subsistence funds, to appropriate part of labour's product. The size of property incomes measures the degree of exploitation. The root of such exploitation lies in private ownership of the means of production, sanctioned by custom, defended by conventional economists, and enforced by capital's power and the coercive apparatus of the state.

FURTHER ITEMS OF RICARDIAN SOCIALIST DOCTRINE

Although their theory of capitalist exploitation is the distinctive feature of Ricardian Socialists' thought, they made other contributions to radical political economy. Despite some individual difference, their ideas can be analysed as a whole:

(i) They attacked the fashionable doctrine of Malthus (1798), which apparently suggested that the working class possesses little hope of increased living standards because population movements prevent wages rising above subsistence level at long-run equilibrium. A rising real wage leads to greater population and hence an excess supply of labour, which persists until wages return to subsistence. This mechanism implies the operation of an 'Iron Law of Wages' that trade unions or legislatures are powerless to suspend. The contemporary abuses of the industrial revolution therefore appeared to be inevitable, the workers' only hopes lying in acceptance of their lot or long-term attempts to limit family size. The Ricardian Socialist reply emphasised that changes in social organisation or technology could affect population; thus the character and availability of contraceptive techniques, the economic status of women and higher living standards are only some influences that may intervene to prevent an increase of subsistence from inducing a rise in the rate of propagation. Moreover, Thompson (1824) pointed to the possible existence of a positive relation between population growth and food supply. When these additional factors are considered, Malthus's theory is seen as relevant to particular situations but misleading as a general hypothesis, particularly under socialism where fewer luxuries would be produced so enabling a larger proportion of total resources to be devoted to the production of food and other essential commodities.

(ii) The Ricardian Socialists buttressed their arguments with statistics collected during the Napoleonic Wars by Colqunhunn (1814), notably his estimates of income distribution, *i.e.* 'more than one fifth of the whole community are unproductive labourers, and these labourers receive from the aggregate labour of the productive classes about one third part of the new product created annually'. Colqunhunn believed that the 'unproductive' promoted the labour of the 'productive', adding that 'without a large proportion of poverty there could be no riches in any country, since riches are the offspring of labour while labour can result only from a state of poverty'. Although Colqunhunn was no radical, he furnished the Ricardian Socialists with statistics whose use in economic debates was a contemporary innovation.

(iii) The Ricardian Socialists possessed an embryonic theory of economic growth linking exchange with the potential for accumulation. They held the romantic notion that before capitalism workers owned the products of their own labour, but they could see that under capitalism the wealth created by using machines goes to capitalists. Therefore automation promotes capital accumulation, while labour's real wage remains stationary due to unequal exchange. Accelerated accumulation thus leads to a relative worsening of the workers' position.

(iv) Gray (1825), was the first Ricardian Socialist to develop a theory of depression in a capitalist economy, so becoming the original English under-consumptionist. He saw two natural limits to production, the exhaustion of finite productive powers and the satisfaction of human needs, both of which were far from realisation in the foreseeable future. Capitalism, however, creates an additional restriction upon output, the requirement for profitability. Consequently capitalists supply only those needs that generate a profit. To overcome this barrier, production should be geared to use, a harbinger of the ideas of the Guild Socialists a century later. Gray maintained that competition limited effective demand by forcing down wages. The resulting 'poverty in the midst of plenty' creates further unemployment, so that a vicious spiral of decline leads to additional falls in demand and subsequently in supply. Competition for reduced custom cuts profits by forcing sales at, or near to, cost price. The depression is characterised by insufficient purchasing power and requires a monetary solution. These ideas represent a pioneering attempt at trade cycle theory.

(v) For the Ricardian Socialists, the concept of socialism did not centre upon class struggle, central state planning or nationalism of the means of production. Instead they emphasised the virtues of collective organisation combined with attacks on the profit motive, private ownership and competition. They believed that cooperative societies subscribed to by workers could supplant the existing individualist structure by productive superiority. Like Owen, they hoped to sponsor collective projects through ruling-class conversion. Even if workers owned their own output, some mechanism is required to prevent the destitution of low or zero producers such as the aged and the sick; again the solution lies in cooperation to achieve some sharing of commodities. The Ricardian Socialists saw everywhere a conflict between private competition and collective benevolence that could be resolved in favour of the latter only by a transformation of the social structure to remedy contemporary evils. The Ricardian Socialists argued that the division of labour facilitated by industrialisation created a growing interdependence whereby no job was more important than any other. Consequently wealth is a communal inheritance and its expansion a communal responsibility.

THE REACTION TO THE RICARDIAN SOCIALISTS: THE ORIGIN OF PROFITS CONTROVERSY

The labour theory of value originally developed in a form providing justification of private property and capitalist incomes. From Petty to Ricardo no economist thought of wage labour as the creator of value, so that alarm spread when the Ricardian Socialists asserted the claim of workers to the total product as a logical deduction from the labour theory of value. As this interpretation appeared to be sanctioned by Ricardo, orthodox economists began to exhibit an ambivalent attitude towards his writing. Many theoretical developments during the 1830s, particularly those related to the origin of profits, arose from efforts to counter the spread of socialist ideas. Theories were constructed which specified that capital also created value, while a few even argued that wage labour created no value at all!

These debates were not confined to academic circles. Conflict between rival economic doctrines gave a powerful stimulus to adult working-class education; Hodgskin played an active part in founding the London Mechanics Institution in 1823, seeking to establish a working-class institution financed solely by working-class money, in conflict with Birkbeck and Place, orthodox followers of Malthus and Ricardo, who were intent on securing middle-class help. Control of the London Mechanics Institution was gained by the orthodox, who were able to obtain greater funds; ultimately it became Birkbeck College, a part of London University. In the 1820s many provisional Mechanics Institutes were formed; whatever their origins, most came under the auspices of middle-class educators, so that their influence was directly non-radical. However, by stimulating discussion, they provided a focus for working-class organisations and the possibility of disseminating Ricardian Socialist ideas.

Although acceptance of the Ricardian Socialists' theory of exploitation was confined to incipient trade unions and radical societies, economists feared its impact, actual or potential; thus Scrope's (1833) reference to persons who 'declaim against capital as the poison of society and robbery of the class of labourers' and Read's (1829) description of Hodgskin's 'mistaken hostility to capital'. It is unsurprising that orthodox defences against the Ricardian Socialists began to appear. These fell in four categories:

(i) The *productivity* theory of profit: Read (1829), the first economist who attempted to answer the Ricardian Socialists without the aid of Malthusian population theory, argued that whenever workers use capital, they do not produce all. He admitted that machinery unaided by labour produces nothing, but claimed that it is the combination of different resources which generates wealth. Within such a conceptual framework, capitalists who organise this combination are 'the greatest of all benefactors to the community'. Read went so far as to argue that 'in effect, though not in law, the labourers are co-proprietors with the capitalists who hire their labour', so that 'want and labour spring from the niggardliness of nature . . . and not from the institution of property'.

(ii) The *abstinence* theory of profit: Longfield (1833) believed that profits are a necessary cost of production, because accumulation occurs only if some individuals abstain from present consumption in order to contribute to a higher future output. Those who so abstain reap the reward of a higher future income as compensation for the immediate loss of consumption. Moreover, this reward is uncertain since business ventures may fail; thus Longfield's abstinence theory foreshadowed the justification of profits in terms of *uncertainty* propounded by later economists such as Knight (1921). Longfield felt that his arguments answered those advocating labour's right to the whole product, whose views, if widespread, would be 'the subversion of civilised society'.

(iii) The *incentive* theory of profit: Scrope (1833) admitted that 'the prevalence of gross misery' inevitably causes criticism of the existing distribution of income, while denying that 'the existence of capital' was its cause. He argued that savings are invested only with the promise of a reward, so that depriving capitalists of profit denies society the production of wealth.

(iv) Most orthodox economists, however, defended capitalist relations of production by *neglect* of Ricardian Socialist views; in Thompson's (1824) words, 'the leaders of the school of *competitive* political economy' were reluctant to discuss 'the system of *cooperative* political economy'.

Those who joined the debate moved away from Ricardo's ideas, because they did not furnish an answer to Ricardian Socialist claims that profit constitutes the appropriation of wealth produced by workers. The labour theory of value embodying such disharmonious implications could no longer be sanctioned. Indeed Scrope argued that Ricardo and his disciples committed 'not merely errors but crimes', because they overthrew 'the fundamental principles of sympathy and common interest that knit society together'. Such views intensified with the increase in social tension in the 1830s exemplified by the campaign for parliamentary reform, the formation of the Grand National Consolidated Trades Union and the rise of Chartism.

The search for an alternative theory of profit ultimately led the orthodox to replace the labour theory of value by utility theory. They redefined labour in terms of the disutility of effort, thus making labour costs commensurate with the cost of capital in the form of a premium to overcome the disutility of abstinence. Therefore, the 1830s witnessed a shift in economic thought towards subjective concepts and the study of exchange relations independent of their social base. The impact of this change dominated orthodoxy after the 1870s, but its tentative beginning in response to the challenge of the Ricardian Socialists occurred forty years earlier.

THE PROBLEMS INVOLVED IN RICARDIAN SOCIALIST THEORY

The Ricardian Socialists perceived that labour is a commodity under capitalism, that workers do not own subsistence funds which are advanced to them by capitalists and that these institutional data produce unequal exchanges in the labour market which favour capitalists. However, evaluation of their theory exposes certain problems, whether labour is regarded as the actual *source* or only as the *measure* of value.

The stronger proposition that labour is the source of all wealth is not self-evident nor a socialist value judgment since it refers to facts about the structure of production and distribution in a capitalist economy. It is a verifiable statement about observed facts only on the assumption that all output can be 'reduced to' (or replaced by) products of unassisted labour. Consequently it faces serious objections as the basis for a theory of capitalist exploitation. Whether or not one accepts the proposition that the first stone-age axe was made by unassisted labour, the physical structure of production since the eighteenth century excludes the necessary assumption as an observable reality. Moreover, an economy where all output is reducible to products of unassisted labour would hardly become capitalist, *i.e.* if corn were produced by unassisted labour and all other commodities by varying combinations of corn and labour, workers need never yield any portion of the net profit to capitalists.

In a capitalist economy where:

(a) no commodities are reducible to products of unassisted labour,

(b) no production is possible without paying profits (given that the basic motivation of capitalist production is accumulation for expanded reproduction, capitalism would never come into existence if profits were not positive and would cease if they permanently fell to zero),

Bose (1975) poses the crucial question: is labour the only source of wealth? He answers in the negative for the following reasons:

(i) The presence of scarce land owned by capitalist landlords: although different kinds of land are physically distinguishable, there can be no general ordering of land in terms of physical attributes such as fertility and location independently of prices and profits. Landlords enjoy a class monopoly over the supply of land, which enables them to deduct rents from real wages and profits even when a competitive land market exists.

(ii) Commodities are not reducible to quantities of directly and indirectly embodied labour determined uniquely by technology, because the combination of direct and indirect labour contained in commodities fluctuates according to the pattern of income distribution between workers and capitalists, *i.e.* the value of the labour contained in a commodity varies with the distribution of income. This statement is untrue only in a non-capitalist economy where the rate of profit is zero at long-run equilibrium.

(iii) The 'reswitching' debate of the 1960s demonstrated that the fluctuations of (ii) are haphazard rather than systematic, *i.e.* the total labour embodied in a commodity may increase or decrease, or first increase and then decrease and then increase again, as distribution shifts in favour of workers at a given technology. The outcome cannot be predicted, so that it becomes impossible to hold that the Ricardian Socialist dictum is even approximately true. Belief that the amount of labour contained in a good varies systematically with the rate of profit is barred by the possibility of reswitching.

(iv) As the rate of profit rises, the value of each component of labour—direct or current; indirect or past—is pulled in opposite directions, so that it moves up or down depending upon which component changes the most. Bose therefore concludes that the statement, 'labour is the only source of wealth', is factually false and cannot provide the basis for a theory of capitalist exploitation.

The weaker proposition that labour is the measure of value faces equally formidable difficulties. Ricardo contended that the price of a commodity was determined by the quantity of direct and indirect labour necessary for its production. The Ricardian Socialists accepted this statement, but without substantial amendment the view that prices are proportional to labour time is an inadequate explanation of the relative price structure in a capitalist economy.

Production is time-consuming, yet workers need consumer goods immediately in order to live and are unable to wait for the proceeds from selling their produce. Consequently capitalists advance at a premium the means to buy goods to their workforce. The money flow of final output, made up of finished ocnsumer and capital goods, exceeds the sum of wages by the volume of profit, which derives from the capitalists' superior ability to wait completion of the production process. When the rate of profit is positive, the price of a commodity depends not only upon the amount of labour required to produce it but also upon the length of time for which that labour is engaged in production. A change in profit rates affects relative prices even though relative quantities of embodied labour remain unchanged:

For example, if X_1 and X_2 are produced in different time periods t_1 and t_2 (of which t_1 is the greater); p = price; w = wage; r = rate of profit; L = labour requirement, then

$$p_1 = wL_1\ (1 + r)\ t_1;\ p_2 = wL_2\ (1 + r)\ t_2;\ \frac{p_1}{p_2} = \frac{(L_1)}{(L_2)}(1 + r)\ t_1 - t_2.$$

Relative prices are not determined by different labour requirements alone unless $t_1 = t_2$ so that the expression $(1 + r)$ vanishes. Goods produced with equal amounts of direct labour but with different amounts of machinery of varying durability cannot sell at the same price. The reply that machines are merely past, embodied labour fails to meet this point, since the present value of a machine exceeds the value of all wages expended on its production in the past by the total of the annual rates of profit. Even if the first piece of capital was made by unassisted labour, from that point onward the labour theory of value as interpreted by the Ricardian Socialists neglects at least one determinant of current prices and is only an approximate account of price formation. Ricardo recognised this problem, but was content to say that embodied labour time was the most important element determining value.

This arbitrary assertion stimulated analysis and economists subsequently attempted to resolve the contradiction created by discrepancies between labour time values and price. Their attempts fell into two broad categories. The first abandoned a labour embodied theory of value even as an approximation and searched for some other account of relative prices. This search led ultimately to marginalism and the post-1870s neoclassical orthodoxy. The other approach recast the labour theory of value to predict systematically divergences between labour values and market prices in the manner Marx later accomplished. The Ricardian Socialists remained content with Ricardo's formulation, so that they suffered from a deficient theory of price determination which created a major weakness in their model of capitalist exploitation. Since every commodity (including labour) has a price in a market economy, the concept of exploitation needs to be incorporated within an analysis of long-run equilibrium prices.

CONCLUSION

The Ricardian Socialists provided an inadequate theory of capitalist exploitation because under capitalism labour cannot be the source of all wealth nor, except on simplifying assumptions, does the labour time embodied in a commodity alone determine its price. Moreover, their proposals to transform the economic organisation were impractical; the principle that workers should receive the full product of their labour ignored the trends towards concentration of production and greater specialisation, while they failed to recognise capitalist power as a major obstacle to realising their plans.

However, the significance of their pioneering models should not be underestimated. Basing their analysis on Ricardo's theories, Colqunhunn's statistics and contemporary evidence of popular distress, they developed the concepts of capitalist exploitation and, implicitly, of surplus value. Although they lacked Marx's comprehensive economic approach, the Ricardian Socialists possess some claim to be his forerunners, since they:

(i) arrived at the concept of all property, but especially financial and industrial capital, as accumulated labour,

(ii) developed an exploitation theory which stimulated further analysis,

(iii) established the idea that unequal exchange[2] rather than population movements maintained wages at a subsistence minimum.

In these ways they perhaps aided Marx, who seems from his writings to have taken Bray (1839), at least, seriously, but even if there was no direct link, they prepared the ground and travelled part of the way. However, Ricardian Socialist theory lacked a number of elements considered crucial by later radicals—notably, a vision of the transition to socialism and the actual or potential phenomena operating to bring this transformation about. Despite such omissions, they provided many concepts and analytical tools for later radicals.

NOTES

1 This abstracts from variations in output per head due to the use of more or less fixed capital relative to labour; otherwise the curves could not be uniquely drawn at a given state of technical knowledge. The model assumes fixed coefficients between capital and labour, but variable coefficients between labour and land.

2 Bray (1839) stressed the role of unemployment, *i.e.* competition for jobs or an excess labour supply, in maintaining the phenomenon of unequal exchange.

4 The Economics of Marx: The Background

'Most of the creations of the intellect or fancy pass away for good after a time that varies between an after-dinner hour and a generation. Some, however, do not. They suffer eclipses, but they come back again, not as unrecognisable elements of a cultural inheritance but in their individual garb and with their personal scars which people may see and touch. These we may call the great ones — it is no disadvantage of this definition that it links greatness to vitality. Taken in this sense, this is undoubtedly the word to apply to the message of Marx'.

J. A. Schumpeter, 1942

'Marxism is an all-embracing science of society, which gives an indispensable sense of understanding the otherwise terrible flux of events. This is one of the reasons why men will both live and die for it'.

J. Strachey, 1956

Karl Marx (1818-83) is the central figure in the history of socialism. That is conceded even by his critics. It is less easy to establish a consensus why he is pre-eminent and it is notoriously impossible to obtain agreement about the significance of his analysis. Marx's life-long friend Friedrich Engels (1820-95) saw Marx's intellectual system as a fusion of three national traditions — German idealist philosophy, French socialist politics and British classical economics — into a coherent theoretical structure, which provided the emerging socialist movement with an ideology encompassing philosophy, history, sociology and economics. Marxism is both an explanation and a critique of capitalism, which challenged the dominant nineteenth-century liberalism not only over individual issues but as an all-embracing vision of society. In the present analysis, Marx's career as a political activist is largely ignored as emphasis is placed upon his economic analysis. This frequently involves discussion of conventionally defined historical, philosophical or sociological topics. Moreover, if the dictum is ever true that a philosophy's whole is greater than the sum of its parts, it applies forcefully to Marxism.

THE ECONOMIC INTERPRETATION OF HISTORY

Marx locates capitalism as one phase in human history, so his economics relates closely to his theory of historical development. He envisages three broad phases of human history:

(i) Initially production was largely agricultural, conducted through the institutions of slavery and feudalism. Humanity had yet to cut its 'umbilical cord' with nature, and social relations were mainly based on personal dependence. This stage of *natural economy* began with the first widespread development of productive forces, the neolithic revolution, when groups which had existed at subsistence level began to intervene in the processes of nature by planting seeds, tending crops and rearing animals to ensure a consistent food supply.

(ii) During the second phase, goods became increasingly produced for sale, initially on an artisan basis but later under capitalist relations. People no longer produce for the direct satisfaction of their own needs, but specialise in making a single commodity for sale and use the proceeds to buy from others. This stage of *commodity production* destroys personal dependency, which is replaced by impersonal reliance on the market. It also cuts the 'umbilical cord' with nature as production becomes chiefly non-agricultural. The consolidation of commodity production in Europe occurred during the industrial revolution because of the systematic use of machinery.

(iii) The third broad stage of human history is *communism* when, after a period of transition, dependence upon the market is replaced by collective control of production by the producers. Nature becomes transformed to satisfy human needs on the basis: 'from each according to his ability, to each according to his need'.

Thus Marx rejects the inevitability of capitalist laws, emphasising their transitory character.

This general historical account demonstrates that for Marx the ultimate purpose of economic activity is the realisation of human freedom, *i.e.* a situation where people live in conformity with their needs and abilities. Marx's 'freedom' contrasts sharply with the liberal definition which refers to an absence of constraints on individual behaviour; although some constraints are seen as inevitable, conventional wisdom holds that they be kept to a minimum. Marx was critical of this negative concept of freedom, because for him the distinctive character of humanity lies in the ability to plan conscious activity directed towards satisfying needs. People do not simply use nature but progressively master it, so that they become capable of creating their own environment and making their own history. They are free to the extent that they consciously control both nature and their social conditions of existence to suit their needs and abilities.

Marx's theory of history centres around the unique significance of labour, which comprises the real cost (*i.e.* expenditure of mental and physical effort) of transforming nature to produce useful objects. It is the necesary condition for all human existence and the activity that creates humanity's character. By acting on the external world and changing it, people simultaneously change their own nature. Labour is social, involving the interdependence of many, so that analysis of economic agents abstracted from their historical environment (for example, the neoclassical concept of utility maximisers) is invalid. History is a process of continuously creating, satisfying and recreating humanity's needs through labour. At a certain point in productive development, perception of new needs and recognition of the possibility of their satisfaction arises. This generates activity designed to realise these potentialities through a new organisation of labour with increased productive power, which generates new needs and a qualitatively new industrial structure. Humanity therefore, is neither fixed and unchanging nor a passive reflector of social circumstances; people make their own history but in specific circumstances which are not of their making.

This economic interpretation of history is compatible with any philosophy. One can accept the doctrine of free will propounded by Aquinas, yet believe that its exercise, restricted by the physical and social environment, produces events in conformity with that environment. Marx's view of history is one hypothesis of what determines the environment, and does not necessarily imply any absence of individual responsibility for behaviour. It holds that historical developments are not random but can be analysed systematically through an evonomic model, whose base consists of two propositions:

(i) Modes of production are the fundamental determinant of social structures which breed actions, attitudes and civilisations; in Marx's phrase 'the hand-mill creates feudal, and the steam-mill creates capitalist, societies'. A mode of production is composed of forces of production (*i.e.* productive technology) and relations of production (*i.e.* the social relationships under which the surplus is produced and its use controlled). This economic *base* of society determines non-economic institutions and processes, which constitute the *superstructure*.

(ii) Modes of production possess a dynamic of their own. They change according to their inherent functioning to produce their successors; to follow Marx's analogy, the hand-mill creates the socio-economic environment in which the adoption of mechanical milling becomes a practical necessity that individuals and groups are powerless to alter. The operation of the steam-mill, however, creates new social groups and attitudes which interact in such a way as to outgrow their institutional infrastructure. Major historical changes occur when the relations of production become a hindrance to developing the forces of production and thus to increasing human control over nature. Each configuration of the relations of production initially stimulates productive forces before becoming an obstacle to their continued expansion.

Therefore Marx believes that historical evolution is propelled by economic change.

Both these propositions provide invaluable working hypotheses, while their synthesis proved an outstanding achievement. Most objections commonly advanced against them fail:

(i) Bernstein (1899) argued that 'men have heads' and so can choose their destiny. Marxists reply that indeed they can but from outlooks that do not constitute independent data but are moulded by the mode of production.

(ii) The economic interpretation of history does not imply that people are motivated wholly by financial motives. Nor does it suggest that religions, philosophies, schools of art and political principles are either reducible to economic factors or are unimportant. Rather it seeks to unveil the economic conditions that shape them and account for their performance. Production and exchange are the basis of every social system, from which major changes result, so that the mode of production ultimately determines the superstructure. Marx sees non-economic ideas as transmission belts through which economic influences become reflected in individual personalities.

(iii) The economic interpretation is often called 'materialistic'. The term is meaningless since Marx's theory is no more materialistic than any attempt to explain history by the means at the command of empirical science.

Despite its strengths, the question arises whether the economis interpretation of history is more than a convenient approximation which explains some events more adequately than others. One minor problem immediately arises: social structures and attitudes are resistant to change and possess different abilities to survive, so that actual institutions always diverge in some degree from anticipations derived from the dominant mode of production. The superstructure generally takes time to adjust to changes in the base, and this adjustment lag is displayed clearly when a durable social structure is transferred from one country to another; for example the system established in Sicily by the Norman Conquest.

Another problem is illustrated by the emergence of feudal landlords in the Kingdom of the Franks during the sixth and seventh centuries, which was a crucial event shaping the structure of society for centuries and influencing conditions of production, wants and technology. They emerged due to the exercise of military leadership by the families who became feudal landlords, yet retained the military function after conquest of new territory. This example does not fit easily into Marx's theory and could be interpreted as pointing in a different direction. A similar example is the influence upon the economic development of the Netherlands of the replacement in the seventeenth century of the merchant oligarchy by the House of Orange. This change, engineered for military reasons in face of an apparent threat from France, was at least a partial cause of the loss of Dutch commercial hegemony.

The American Civil War constitutes a more recent test-case. The traditional view was that the essential quarrel dividing the Union in 1860 centred upon slavery; the North detested it while the South glorified it as the basis of its society, so that the two were unable to co-exist and the Civil War inevitably occurred. Marxists, such as the Beards (1927) attacked this conventional wisdom by transposing the conflict to a struggle of economic interests. They placed in opposition not slavery and liberty, but the agrarian economy of the South relying upon free trade and the nascent capitalism of the North requiring tariffs to protect infant industries from foreign competition. This theory emphasised issues that were previously neglected, yet a number of problems arise when relying upon it as an exclusive explanation. Thus at the moment of decision the capitalists of the North clamoured for peace, while the war fervour in the South is inexplicable as the reaction to a purely economic menace, especially as the southern states were prospering materially. It seems likely to have been at least partly a reply to an ethical indictment and a feeling that by retaining slavery the South cut itself adrift from the development of Western civilisation. Moreover, the Beards treated the Abolitionists as insignificant, stressing their small numbers and the fact that until the Civil War their politics excluded them from office, but ignoring the dynamism of their ideas. A generation before the Civil War the first Abolitionists endured persecution in the North. Their ultimate success shows that numbers are not always decisive, since the struggle by a few of ethical conviction can alter an environment.

A crucial issue for any general theory of history is to explain why capitalism originated in Western Europe. Under capitalism workers are separated from their means of production and do not own finished products, so that they live by selling their labour power in exchange for a wage. Such a system never occurred on a large scale until eighteenth-century Europe for reasons not immediately apparent, since the numerical expansion of merchant petty commodity production was at least as great elsewhere, for example in the Mogul Empire in India, the Islamic Empire, China and Japan. However, only in Western Europe did the agricultural surplus permanently take the form of money rent. Other economies rested on irrigation which enabled the development of an intensive agriculture that in turn caused rapid population growth. Competition from cheap labour, or the predominance of slave labour, prevented large-scale mechanisation of crafts. Medieval Europe possessed less fertile soil, so that the density of population was lower with consequently less state control; the absolute state was related to irrigation agriculture, which required strict administration and centralisation of the social surplus. In Western Europe the supremacy of movable wealth over land was established by the sixteenth century, while the state became subject to public debt. Therefore few obstacles to the accumulation of capital remained. From the eleventh century onwards capital accumulation enriched the bourgeoisis, which progressively freed itself from the control exercised by feudal landlords and the state, and eventually used the government apparatus to promote its ends. In other pre-capitalist civilisations arbitrary confiscation of profit by the state was a continual threat and a periodic occurrence. Only in Japan, whose pirate merchants accumulated capital from the fourteenth century onwards as government authority broke down, did bourgeois supremacy permit a later evolution of capitalism. Thus the economic interpretation of history can provide a comprehensive account of the rise of capitalism in Western Europe.

Certain episodes problematic to Marx's theory of history can be found, but they have to be sought for and can be accommodated by admitting some measure of interaction between the sphere of production and other areas of social life. However, if the strictness of the one-way relation it asserts is modified, the economic interpretation of history becomes one partial hypothesis or gives way to a model of greater explanatory power. Neither its rank as an achievement nor its utility as an analytical tool is thereby impaired. Marx's vision of historical transition emphasises the development of productive forces *within* a system of social relations until they outgrow it, come into conflict with it and ultimately burst its bounds.

THE THEORY OF SOCIAL CLASS

Marx and Engels stated in *The Communist Manifesto* that history is a series of class struggles (for example, masters v. slaves, lords v. serfs, master craftsmen v. apprentices and journeymen, capitalists v. workers), each successive stage evolving from its predecessor. Therefore the theory of social class complements the economic interpretation of history, as classes are the crucial actors propelling historical development. The nature of class control over production of the surplus differs between economies, but is the basic relationship upon which the social structure rests.

The concept of class conflict distinguishes Marxist analysis from most conventional social science. Marx's theory of social class rests upon three basic propositions:

(i) Classes are groups of people sharing a common relationship to the means of production. In class-divided economies (*i.e.* all since primitive communism), there are two basic classes; the owners and the non-owners of the inanimate prerequisites for production. Thus the class structure of capitalism may be reduced to the capitalists who own, and the workers who do not own, the means of production.

(ii) The position of these two classes in the productive process makes their interests necessarily antagonistic, because those owning productive property can exploit those without it. Exploitation has a precise meaning for Marx, referring to the mechanism whereby the dominant class extracts surplus labour from the subordinate class. Workers retain only part of their output, the rest being appropriated by capitalists.

(iii) The resulting class conflict generates economic and political mechanisms that implement the tendency of the mode of production to revolutionise itself from within.

The struggle between capitalists and workers emerges from an economic organisation in which the means of production are owned by capitalists, who can force labour to take employment on their terms. The operation of labour markets places individual workers in an inferior bargaining position when negotiating wages and conditions of work with their employers.[1] The worker enters into employment because social conditions offer no other way of obtaining a livelihood. The capitalist, on the other hand, sets in motion the labour process as a vehicle for the expansion of capital and the creation of a profit.

The existence of capitalism implies that the majority lack access to the means of production, thus suffering financial although not legal compulsion to sell their labour. An economy where individuals own the capital they work with is only possible when small-scale operations yield maximum efficiency, but much of modern industry requires costly and elaborate techniques to reap economies of scale. Therefore large amounts of capital are needed to start a business. Such amounts— beyond the reach of most of the population—have increased with progressive mechanisation; Baran (1957) estimated that between 1890 and 1940 the initial investment involved in establishing a viable U.S. manufacturing enterprise increased on average in real terms about tenfold. This barrier to entry adds a monopoly element onto profits, the size of which varies between industries according to the volume of capital needed to set up a new enterprise.

The working class, unable to achieve such an investment, finds its job opportunities, methods of work and distribution by area, industry and occupation determined by the ongoing process of accumulation. It is employed, dismissed, flung into various parts of the economic system and expelled from others, not in accord with its own will or activity but with the movement of capital. Therefore class conflict is not solely concerned with distribution where capitalists lose what workers gain, but focusses also upon conditions of employment. Nor is the struggle reserved for markets and factories; state intervention, media appeals and political movements all play a role. Wealth yields control over the resources that are put to social use, but this control is exercised on the basis of individual self-interest.

Such dominance deriving from capital ownership is not universal but is of fairly recent origin. Thus the capital possesed by pre-industrial communities, such as North American Indians, was negligible in volume and easy to replace. More crucial to their livelihood was accumulated knowledge of soils, seasons, food, fibre plants, mechanical expedients and animal behaviour, so that viable economic agents were not solitary cultivators or hunters but collective units. Knowledge was the product of the whole group and no great significance was attached to capital ownership. With industrialisation the capital required to put group knowledge into effect grows larger and its acquisition increasingly difficult, so that ownership becomes crucial. In effect, owners of finance are able to appropriate group knowledge and its application. Thus the terms in which an entity of capital is defined cannot be physical but are attributes of ownership, *i.e.* legal rights, contract and sale. Consequently capitalists monopolise a portion of the intangible assets of the community and own the material contrivances by which technical progress is put into effect.

Marx adds a further refinement; he claims that capitalism undermined its own foundation by progressively eliminating small-scale owners of the means of production. Statistical evidence supports this claim. In the early nineteenth century around eighty per cent of the non-slave population in the U.S.A. owned the means of produciton with which they worked, whereas today approximately the same proportion consists of wage or salaried workers. Their living standards have risen dramatically, but their class has become proletarian with the gradual diminution of the individual entrepreneur as the fulcrum of industrial organisation. The exchange of labour power has been occurring since antiquity, but a substantial class of employed workers did not form in Europe until the fourteenth century and has constituted a majority for little more than a hundred years in a few countries. The proportion of the U.S. population that was self-employed declined from four-fifths in the early ninetenth century to one-third (1870), one-fifth (1940) and one-tenth (1970). The rapidity of this transformation demonstrates the overwhelming tendency of capitalism to convert other forms of work into wage labour.

Marx believes that the successor to capitalism will be communism, where class formations based on ownership of the means of production are eliminated. Class and the possibility of class conflict will be abolished, so that no antithesis to communism arises. Communism originates from capitalism, being a product of forces to which capitalism gives birth and it is, by definition, the only possible kind of classless society excepting subsistence agrarian groups. It is brought about in a revolutionary situation, where the working class attempts to abolish private property thereby rendering its propertyless condition the general one; once the proletariat comprising a majority disappears as a separate class it becomes possible to speak of a common interest. Workers' revolutionary potential is realised only with a conjunction of objective conditions (a crisis of capitalism) and subjective awareness (class consciousness).

In addition to many specific insights, the overall achievement of Marx's theory of social class is to emphasise that economic relationships possess a social character. This emphasis conflicts with the methodology of non-Marxists, which assumes that social reality in its most important economic aspects reflects the preferences of individuals interacting through procedures of choice with objectively given resource and technology constraints. However, individual tastes are an unsuitable foundation for eocnomic models, because in any logically consistent theory the exogenous variables must be stable, either remaining unchanged or moving in accord with well-defined laws. Orthodox economists present no case for making such assumptions about individual preferences; rather they assert that individuals choose to do (or have) what they prefer to do (or have), which is circular reasoning unless hypotheses of the determination of tastes, and changes in them, are developed. No such economic hypotheses exist, yet until they do, many orthodox concepts disintegrate; to take one example, if the utility derived from consumption of a particular commodity depends on individuals' previous consumption, it becomes impossible to determine whether they are better off with a history of high or low consumption. Heroin and classical music are both relevant cases, but non-Marxists lack a definition of welfare that enables them to indicate, without value judgments, the preferability of addiction to music rather than heroin. The lack of any explanation of the determination of individual preferences reduces orthodox consumer theory to a set of tautologies. To overcome this dilemma, a model of individual tastes must be constructed or a different approach developed in which the formation of preferences is not centrally important.

Non-Marxist economists have been slow to recognise the existence of social classes; they classify the agents they analyse, but the categories obtained (*e.g.* landlords, rentiers, workmen) are simply sets of individuals displaying some common characteristic. However, 'individuals' exist within a class under certain productive relations generated by a particular mode of production. By treating all economic agents as individuals making choices, the orthodox fail to perceive that the range of choice available (or its absence) depends upon the chooser's class position. They also ignore the fact that freedom of choice often characterises capitalism by its presence in trivial aspects and its absence in important ones. Thus workers possess a degree of choice concerning which capitalist they work for, but cannot for financial reasons decide not to work at all; similarly capitalists can choose where to invest their capital, but they must invest profitably to retain their position. Individuals are potentially equal at the level of exchange, but within production they are unequal and bound by capitalist class relations. Orthodox economics, by concentrating upon the former, emphasises the freedom of the market and fails to uncover the relations of production which influence economic development. So implicitly it is ideologically supportive of capitalism, while analytically it fails to explain why different economic formations exist and how transition from one to another occurs.

To reveal the relations of production, a class analysis concerned with the interaction of groups defined in relation to their role in the labour process is required. Orthodox economists tend to view the social character of economic relationships as natural and harmonious, but economics for Marx centres upon the determination of these relationships and their development. Therefore disagreement exists between Marxists and non-Marxists about the scope of economics and its appropriate level of abstraction; orthodoxy takes as given the institutional data that are the foundation of Marx's analysis, which places a sociological fact (class monopoly of the ownership of the means of production) at its foundation.

A number of objections are advanced against Marx's theory of social class:

(i) Analysis based upon classes depends crucially upon the definition of class adopted. Interpretation of the mechanism of social change is very different, depending upon whether a racial theory (for example Gobineau (1855) saw history in terms of the struggle of races) or a division of labour theory (for example Durkheim (1933) viewed class antagonisms as a conflict between vocational groups)[2] of classes is adopted. Even if definitional agreement is reached, different analyses flow from different conceptions of class interest and from different opinions about how class action manifests itself. Marxist classes are stratified by ownership, or exclusion from ownership, of the means of production; two classes exist, that possessing property and that compelled to sell its labour. Intermediate groups (*e.g.* artisans, farmers, professionals) are acknowledged but are seen as anomalies that become 'proletarianised' during capitalist development. Rifts within each class may occur in particular situations, but ownership of the means of production polarises society into two strata, a view borne out by available statistics concerning the distribution of income.[3]

(ii) It is sometimes argued that business achievement is not the sole route to social eminence, so that ownership of the means of production is not the only determinant of positions in the power hierarchy. However, in the long run status is maintained only when reflected in corresponding economic positions, although at any one time rigidities and anachronisms exist.

(iii) It is claimed that Marx exaggerated the antagonisms between capitalists and workers. Under capitalism, conflict and cooperation are both ubiquitous and normally inseparable. This weakens the dynamics of Marx's theory, for if class struggle is the subject of history and the means of realising communism, class relations need to be inherently antagonistic. To capitalists, wages are both a cost and a source of purchasing power; the classes conflict over distribution, yet each shares an interest in maintaining production and increasing national income. Whether cooperation or antagonism is the dominant facet of class relations, in particular circumstances and generally, is a controversial issue. Both are always present and each dominant group endeavours to represent its interests as society-wide, but examples of class cooperation are widespread; thus in most twentieth-century wars nation dominated class, while in peace the capitalists and workers of developed economies have each, in varying degrees, exploited the underdeveloped. Moreover, cross-class alignments occur; members of the bourgeoisie may lead working-class movements which much of the proletariat is reluctant to join. A variety of outcomes is possible, but it is doubtful whether the complexity of graduations in any actual situation violates the underlying insight of Marx's perception.

(iv) As ownership is the constituent characteristic of Marx's social classes, 'primitive accumulation' becomes a vital issue *i.e.* the methods by which capitalists acquired the resources that enabled them initially to achieve their position. Marx rejects the idea that capitalists possess superior intelligence or energy in working and saving. The bulk of accumulation comes from profits, and thus presupposes profits, but no rate of profit could induce the saving required to secure economies of scale if workers are free to consume the full equivalent of their product. Marx's theory of primitive accumulation stresses the role of force, robbery and subjugation, but fails to explain how capitalists obtained the power to rob and subjugate. He believes it essential for the logic of capitalism that it originated from feudalism, defined as a reign of force in which exploitation and subjugation already occurred. So capitalist exploiters simply replaced feudal ones. Where landlords actually became industrialists the problem is solved, yet the two groups did not necessarily coincide. It is difficult to explain all primitive accumulation without resorting to non-Marxist hypotheses; even when account is taken of robbery which was crucial for building up commercial capital through such enterprises as Pheonician wealth and English piracy, successful robbery rests ultimately on the personal superiority of the robbers. If this is conceded, a non-Marxist theory of social stratification presents itself.

The development of capitalist relations of production was long and complex. They matured in Britain for over two centuries before the industrial revolution and had two transitional phases. Firstly, the small producers became emancipated from feudal bonds and secondly, they were separated from ownership of the means of production. A number of factors were crucial to this transformation, including growth of population, direct eviction, indebtedness, development of production for the market, the prevalence of monetary exchange and a series of technical inventions harnessing mechanical power. In the late eighteenth century natural population increase plus recruits from surplus agricultural labour supply furnished a proletariat to work with the accumulating capital. In such specific historical circumstances Marxism accounts for primitive accumulation by the different endowments of resources, but it is doubtful whether it can provide an adequate explanation otherwise or develop models indicating the determinants of these differential endowments.

(v) Given the difficulties posed by primitive accumulation, Schumpeter (1942) argued that Marx's theory of social class becomes redundant because the methods of primitive accumulation also account for later accumulation. He claimed that primitive accumulation continues throughout the capitalist era, so that the theory of class cannot be considered satisfactory except in its analysis of processes in a distant past. This objection fails to meet Marx's case. Individual saving by the thrifty may be vital for primitive accumulation when the minimum sum required to start an enterprise is small, but such saving proves inadequate for further accumulation whose source is overwhelmingly profits from existing capital. Only those possessing capital and receiving profits can save substantially. Schumpeter confused the conditions giving birth to a mode of production (or new units within it) with those of its renewal; even if every firm originated in hard work, capitalism as a system is not thereby justified, because it is inherently exploitative once in operation.

(vi) Belief in a 'Managerial Revolution', if correct, refutes Marx's theory of class. It is often argued that ownership of the means of production has become divorced from their control, so that classes defined by ownership no longer generate social conflict. Hired managers now make the key decisions affecting workers' lives, but they are recruited from all sections of the population and take such decisions in a socially responsible way,[4] while the search for profit is merely one of a number of corporate objectives. Belief in a 'Managerial Revolution' rests upon two assumptions: that a divorce between ownership and control has actually occurred, and that such a divorce implies an end to class warfare.

The weight of empirical and theoretical evidence against the existence of a 'Managerial Revolution' is heavy. In Britain and other advanced capitalist economies, most shareholders in large companies possess small stockholdings, so that a minority control the majority of share capital. Dispersed shareholding facilitates domination by the few, particularly when they form a coherent group through family connections or interlocking directorships; in 1970 ninety-three per cent of the U.K. population over the age of twenty-five owned no income-yielding assets: eighty per cent of these assets were held by one per cent of the adult population.[5] In such circumstances company chairmen and directors are chosen from within the ranks of a largely self-perpetuating oligarchy, while managers are a tightly-knit group overlapping capitalist owners. Moreover, managers in total tend to own a substantial proportion of shares.

Irrespective of management's origins and personal motives, market logic compels its decisions to conform with capitalist criteria. As managers possess the formal status of employees, the financial failure of their enterprises conflicts with their ambitions. Nor was the individual entrepreneur, with whom the modern corporation is contrasted, necessarily a profit maximiser for many adopted paternalist policies. Because of their wealth, social background, but above all their corporate function, managers remain members of the capitalist class and count among the staunchest defenders of private property. Divisions of opinion occur among capitalists, but these fail to transform fundamentally the social structure.

(vii) The doctrine of 'embourgeoisement' holds that the rise in real income and the spread of status symbols leads to working-class assimilation into the middle class. Technical progress creates changes in the occupational distribution, towards greater demand for more skill and a consequent reduction in the number of low-paid workers. Higher incomes, the increased importance of education[6] and greater mobility generate fluidity in class distinctions. Marx's definition of the working class, *i.e.* those who do not own or otherwise enjoy proprietory access to the means of production, embraces almost all the population yet encompasses occupational strata of diverse forms. Therefore the workers' class position is eroded by autonomous market and technological changes rather than conscious political and social action.

Lockwood and Goldthorpe's (1968) study of the 'affluent worker' found little support for these assertions. When manual workers obtain relatively high incomes they tend to suffer greater deprivation at work in the form of overtime, shifts, low career mobility and greater susceptibility to unemployment. A higher standard of living for the majority must not be confused with more egalitarian distribution; thus the Diamond Commission's statistics suggest that in 1972-3 the richest one per cent possessed as much income as the poorest thirty per cent and that the richest fifty per cent received over three quarters of total income. Nor should it be assumed that technical progress necessarily requires a more skilled labour force. Braverman (1974), arguing from a Marxist perspective, presents the opposite case that changes in productive technology progressively 'deskilled' much of the workforce. Thus the mental processes involved in clerical work are rendered routine or reduced to so small an element in the labour process that the speed with which the manual portion of the operation can be performed is dominant. Clerks are placed on an equivalent footing to manual workers, so that the traditional distinction between white- and blue-collared labour represents echoes of a past situation largely irrelevant to the contemporary world.

The divide in work experiences and life chances between manual and non-manual employees became blurred with the proletarianisation of the lower professions and office jobs. The growth of white-collar labour hailed by anti-Marxists as demonstrating the falsity of Marx's theory of social class involves the creation of a large proletariat in a different form.

Rather than constituting an intermediate middle class, this group has lost former relative superiorities over manual workers in both pay and conditions of employment. The designation of administrative, professional and technical workers as a new class, *e.g.* by Galbraith (1958), raises problems. The formerly self-employed middle class occupied that position by virtue of its place outside the polarised class structure, but the new class by contrast is part of the process of capital accumulation and possesses characteristics of both capital and labour. It receives a minor share of capital's prerogatives and rewards, but in its subordination as hired labour it resembles the proletarianised condition. Even where recruitment by achievement replaces recruitment by ascription, achievement in conventional terms seems to be a class characteristic. A limited amount of social mobility occurs, but its major effect may be to legitimise inequality by limiting discontent.

(viii) The last point demonstrates that the objective existence of Marx's social classes may not be reflected in the state of class consciousness, *i.e.* the understanding and activities of a class. The *absolute expression* of class consciousness is a durable attitude on the part of a class towards its position in society. Its *long-term relative expression* is contined in the slowly changing traditions, experiences, education and organisation of the class. Its *short-term relative expression* is a dynamic complex of moods and sentiments affected by circumstances, which may change rapidly in periods of crisis. These three expressions of class consciousness are related; changes of mood ventilate the underlying reservoir of attitudes. A class cannot exist without in some degree manifesting a consciousness of itself as a group with common problems, interests and prospects, although this manifestation may for long periods be weak, confused and subject to manipulation by other classes.

CONCLUSION

Marxisim is a fusion of three national traditions, a synthesis of philosophy, politics and economics, and socialism's answer to liberalism. Through his theory of classes, Marx defined capitalism sociologically, *i.e.* by the institution of private ownership of the means of production, but to understand its mechanics an economic theory is required to show how the sociological data embodied in class behaviour work out in economic terms (*e.g.* profits, wages and investment), and how they generate the economic development that eventually destroys its own institutional framework while simultaneously creating the conditions for the emergence of another social world. The economic interpretation of history, the theory of social class and analysis of the profit economy marshal facts not as isolated concepts but as part of the overall Marxist vision. Having considered the economic interpretation of history and the theory of social class, we now turn to the more 'economic' aspects of the synthesis, always however viewing production in term sof power relations manifested through class.

NOTES

1 Burkitt (1980) analysed in detail the various factors operating in the labour market which bring about labour's bargaining weaknesses.
2 Today classes are frequently defined in relation to ranked groups and status evaluations rather than to the inequality of ownership. Thus the Registrar-General's definition of socio-economic class shifts emphasis from the mode of production to the structure of occupational hierarchies and the determinants of an individual's place within them.
3 Atkinson (1972) found that the richest one per cent of the British population own at least a quarter, and the richest five per cent at least a a half, of total personal wealth. The distribution of income from property is even more unequal, with five per cent of all adults receiving no less than ninety-two per cent of such income, and ninety-three per cent of adults in 1970 owning no shares or government bonds. Although the distribution of wealth and property income appears to be more unequal in Britain than in most other developed capitalist economies, a similar pattern emerges elsewhere. Indeed it is likely that most statistics understate the degree of inequality due to legal and illegal forms of tax evasion.
4 Patten (1907) developed the concept of 'The Soulful Corporation'.
5 Westergaard and Resler (1975) provided detailed statistics on this point.
6 Often termed significantly 'investment in human capital'.

5 The Economics of Marx: Tools of Analysis

Marx bases his economic analysis not on individuals but on the social relations between them, so that his ultimate concerns are people in society and the process of social change. Humans differ from animals in that they change their environment which is not solely determined by nature. Labour is the means whereby natural conditions are transformed; initially it focusses upon the provision of subsistence, but in industrial economies more hours are worked than are necessary for survival. The basis of material progress is the surplus time beyond that required for subsistence, which can be used in leisure or to generate additional production. These considerations suggest that labour is the active creator of wealth and that its allocation is crucial for development. Consequently Marx believes that the purpose of economics is to explore the relations under which the surplus is produced and its use controlled.[1] A reformulated labour theory of value is the foundation of his attempt to uncover these relations.

MARX'S REFORMULATION OF THE LABOUR THEORY OF VALUE

Most late eighteenth- and early nineteenth-century economists in Britain held some variant of the labour theory of value. Ricardo (1817) stated its central proposition as follows: 'the value of every commodity is (in perfect competition and at equilibrium) proportional to the quantity of labour embodied in it, providing that this labour is used in accord with existing standards of productive efficiency (the socially necessary amount of labour)'. This quantity is measured in labour hours, with different qualities of work reduced to a single standard by the time taken to acquire a skill. The labour embodied in a commodity includes that required to create subsidiary goods entering into its production, while capital is defined as the product of past, stored-up labour. Ricardo used the term 'value' synonymously with 'price' and thought that commodities exchange at prices which reflect the relative amounts of labour embodied in them.

However, the labour theory of value encounters problems if used in this manner to determine relative prices. The orthodox critique of Marx follows Bohm-Bawerk (1896) in arguing that Marx did not satisfactorily derive prices from labour values. The major difficulties of Ricardo's theory are these:

(i) it provides a complete explanation only under perfect competition, since in other market structures relative prices vary with the degree of monopoly and the excess profit thus attained.

(ii) It encounters obstacles when labour is heterogenous. It accounts for skill variations by the time taken to acquire them through training, but differential natural ability, whatever its origin, is less easily quantifiable in terms of hours. It requires additional assumptions, so that problems of measurement become severe.

(iii) Ricardo's theory underemphasises, without completely ignoring, the influence of demand. Consequently its analysis is sometimes convoluted; for example, few accept that diamonds command a high price solely because their scarcity causes a large amount of labour to be devoted to their discovery and production.

(iv) Expectations may cause the price of a good to fluctuate through speculation and stockpiling, although the amount of labour embodied in it remains unaltered. Ricardo's theory contains no account of what determines expectations and so provides at best a partial account of the price structure.

(v) Gifts of nature owned by capitalist landlords are neglected. Although different kinds of land can be physically distinguished, no general ordering in terms of fertility and locational advantage can be constructed independently of prices and profits. Landlords as a class enjoy an institutional monopoly which enables them to deduct rent from real wages even when a competitive land market exists. Therefore prices may diverge from labour values.

(vi) Applying Ricardo's theory leads to conundrums:

(a) It becomes indeterminate when a commodity can be produced by two equally profitable techniques embodying different amounts of labour. Some capitalists use one technique and some the other, but which determines price?

(b) Potentially it yields negative values when joint production occurs. The labour time embodied in each commodity can only be derived when it is possible to produce them singly. However, if the total time embodied in a joint labour process is less than in a non-joint one, a negative value for one commodity is obtained by subtracting the non-joint labour value from the joint two product labour value.

These anomalies arise because capitalists take decisions on the basis of costs rather than labour time, so that profit maximisation does not necessarily correspond to labour time minimisation. These problems cannot be resolved without introducing an additional principle into the labour theory of value.

(vii) The time taken to produce commodities is crucial to price determination. If commodities exchange at prices proportional to embodied labour time, the annual rate of profit is lower for a capitalist whose capital is committed over a long period than for one whose capital is used up faster, even if the total labour time embodied is the same for each. The more slowly produced good must be priced higher, since otherwise capitalists will forward no funds for its production. Because commodities tie up capital for different times, prices cannot be determined solely by labour time. Where competition equalises the rate of profit on capital per time period, different turnovers modify the determination of price by embodied labour. At least two factors affect relative prices; the time that capital is fixed in a specific usage and the relative quantity of labour embodied in a commodity's production.

(viii) The time pattern taken by stored-up labour is also crucial. If the temporal structure of past labour (*i.e.* capital) varies between commodities, discounting is necessary to reflect the varying contribution of labour at different stages of the past, *i.e.* account must be taken of the greater productivity of last year's labour which produced up to date equipment compared to that of twenty years ago whose output currently approaches obsolescence. Therefore when the time structure of past labour varies between commodities, further deviations of relative prices from labour values occur.

Ricardo was aware of some of these difficulties, but made the arbitrary assumption that embodied labour time was the most important element in price determination. His theory represents only a broad tendency, as over the long run goods embodying much labour habitually sell for more than those with little (*e.g.* airliners and bicycles; turbogenerators and electric kettles), while general price movements tend to conform to changes in labour values (*e.g.* the fall in the price of primary products relative to the price of manufactures during the nineteenth century). To obtain a more precise hypothesis of price determination, two alternative approaches are possible:

(i) to abandon the labour theory of value. Historically, this approach produced neoclassical economics, which analyses price in terms of the interaction between relative demand and relative costs. By discarding the labour theory of value and with it the notion that labour was the active agent involved in the creation of wealth, neoclassicals view production as the result of mutual cooperation between several factors.

(ii) to recast the labour theory of value in order to achieve greater precision. Marx admits that prices deviate from labour values but claims that they do so in a systematic, and therefore in a predictable, way.

Marx seeks to answer two questions. To the first, the qualitative problem of value (*i.e.* what social property allows commodities to be reduced to a common denominator of exchange), he argues that the value of commodities is determined by the amount of abstract labour socially necessary for their production. To the second, the quantitative problem of value (*i.e.* what determines the numerical ratios at which commodities exchange), he answers that prices are set by transformed quantities of socially necessary labour time. Abstract labour is defined as purposive human activity undertaken in abstraction from the specific characteristics of the jobs actually performed, while socially necessary labour occupies the time technologically required to produce a given article in the quantity demanded.

Marx believes that prices can be explained *in terms of* labour quantities, but certain misunderstandings must be clarified:

(i) His theory is not based on the assumption that labour constitutes the only factor of production. He recognises the role of natural resources and machinery in augmenting material wealth, and it would be inconsistent to argue that capital is worthless while advocating its collective ownership as the key to social transformation.

(ii) His theory does not rest on the moral precept that commodities ought to exchange on the basis of the labour embodied in them. He attempts to construct an analytical tool rather than formulate a normative proposition.

(iii) Unlike Ricardo, he does not state that commodities exchange at prices proportional to the amounts of labour embodied in them. He acknowledges divergences but supplies an explanation, *i.e.* that many commodities must be sold at prices higher or lower than their labour values in order to yield a uniform rate of profit.

In a competitive capitalist economy the rate of profit tends to equality over all industries, because profitability differences stimulate movements of capital towards the more, and away from the less, remunerative sectors until such discrepancies disappear. But a uniform rate of profit is consistent with prices proportional to socially necessary labour time only when the organic composition of capital is equal in every industry. The organic composition of capital is the number of labour hours used up as raw materials, intermediate products and fixed capital depreciation (constant capital or C) divided by the number of hours production workers consume represented by the flow of wage and salary payments (variable capital or V). Marx considers that constant capital adds to the value of the goods it produces only the value of the labour time embodied in its own production. Variable capital possesses the unique potentiality of being able to create output of a greater value than its own; labour power not only reproduces its own value but in addition generates surplus value (S). Under non-competitive capitalism, the rate of surplus value ($\frac{S}{V}$) and the rate of profit ($\frac{S}{C+V}$) are greatest in industries where production is most labour intensive, *i.e.* where the organic composition of capital ($\frac{C}{V}$) is lowest.

However, competition operates to establish a uniform rate of profit by redistributing the mass of surplus value until the value of $\frac{S}{V}$ in each industry offsets the differences in the capital-labour ratio. The price structure which yields a uniform rate of profit can be calculated from a series of simultaneous equations; competition brings about a fall in the prices of products using a high ratio of living labour (*i.e.* a low $\frac{C}{V}$), while the prices of products using a low ratio of living labour (*i.e.* a high $\frac{C}{V}$) rise. The process continues until the rate of profit is equalised. Therefore labour values — the amount of socially necessary abstract labour embodied in a good — require transformation according to the organic composition of capital, in order to determine price. Commodity prices are exactly proportional to labour values only when their organic composition of capital is equal to the average organic composition over all industry.

The need to transform labour values in terms of the organic composition of capital does not vitiate the labour theory of value, since long-run equilibrium prices diverge *systematically* from labour values. With above average organic composition of capital, prices exceed labour values; for under average organic composition of capital, prices settle below labour values; and where the organic composition of capital equals the economy-wide average, prices and labour values are identical. Therefore, Ricardo's labour theory of value needs modification to provide a coherent explanation of price determination. Supply and demand movements can cause relative price changes, but Marx sees these as deviations around a norm set by equilibrium prices systematically derived from labour values.

Marx establishes a theoretical connection between the prices and labour values of commodities, but his numerical attempts to solve this transformation problem by example are unsatisfactory, because he fails to transform the labour value of inputs as well as outputs. On this basis, Bohm-Bawerk (1896) dismissed Marx's reformulation and prophesied the demise of his system, 'which has a past and a present but no abiding future'. Bohm-Bawerk failed to consider whether Marx's transformation problem can be solved by an alternative mathematical treatment. In fact it can; Bortkiewicz (1907) solved the relevant set of simultaneous equations for three sectors, while Seton (1957), a non-Marxist, demonstrated a general solution for any number of commodities (the N-product case) and provided formal proof of its validity. Such a demonstration is implicit in the equations, deriving prices from the conditions of production and the ratio of profits to wages, constructed by Sraffa (1960).

The solution amounts to asserting that under capitalism a functional relation exists between labour values and equilibrium prices expressed as:

$$\text{Price of a Commodity} = C + V + \frac{C + V}{\Sigma (C + V)} (\Sigma S)$$

where C = the value of used-up machinery and raw materials;
V = the value of labour power;
S = surplus value;
$\Sigma C + V$ = the aggregate capital (constant plus variable) employed over the whole economy;
ΣS = the aggregate surplus value produced over the whole economy.

All items on the right of the equation can be expressed in terms of transformed quantities of embodied labour, so that a direct relationship exists between labour values and equilibrium prices of production. Divergencies between them are not random but systematic and therefore predictable. It is this assertion that distinguishes Marx's labour theory of value from that of Ricardo.

Any attack upon Marx's reformulation on the grounds of over-simplification is misconceived but a more valid criticism may be that it is an unnecessarily complex theory of price determination. However, one of its strengths is its concentration upon labour as the active creator of the material basis of life; by arguing that land, raw materials, equipment and plant merely cooperate with the labour time that is exchanged and employed, attention is directed to the forces that stimulate a rapid growth in labour's productivity. The labour theory of value and the marginalist alternative cannot be compared simply as rival explanations of relative prices since they constitute fundamentally different conceptualisations of the entire economic process.

The labour theory of value as reformulated by Marx provides a determinate account of the price structure but is complicated to use in practice. Contemporary radicals accord this topic a lower priority than do conventional economists and argue that Marx's model is better equipped to analyse the operation and development of capitalism. The labour theory of value enables a distinction to be drawn between the productivity of machinery created by past labour and the ability of its owners to appropriate part of its product as profit. In Robinson's (1942) words: 'whether we choose to say that capital is productive or that capital is necessary to make labour productive is not very important . . . what is important is to say that owning capital is not a productive activity'. This distinction links directly to Marx's theory of exploitation, which incorporates capitalist exploitation into a general equilibrium theory of prices.

MARX'S THEORY OF EXPLOITATION

Marx distinguishes *exploitation* (extraction of surplus labour in the form of surplus value) from *oppression* (control of some people by others). He explains the existence of a net return to capital by the phenomenon of exploitation which is not accidental but results from the inherent logic of capitalism.

Theories of the origin of profit divide into two categories:

(i) those that regard profit as a residual from the net social product. Marx's theory falls into this category, for surplus value is seen as a costless gain for capitalists,

(ii) those that consider profit as the exchange equivalent of some specific contribution to production incurring a 'real cost' (*e.g.* abstinence, the bearing of uncertainty). Such theories place profits and wages on an equivalent footing by relating the structure of inequality to individual costs and sacrifices rather than to social processes.

Marxists believe that the second type of theory is inadequate, because it fails to reveal the characteristics of capitalism from which profits derive, particularly the class monopoly of ownership of the means of production. Profit could be eliminated only if complete freedom of entry to capitalist ranks exists. This requires either:

(i) that individuals are able to borrow the requisite funds at the prevailing rate of interest, or

(ii) that production can be efficiently undertaken in units possessing small stocks of capital.

The first condition is unrealistic, while the second applies only to a few trades given the existence of modern production techniques and associated economies of scale. The scarcity of individuals commanding sufficient funds for industrial efficiency maintains a positive rate of profit.

The *rate of surplus value* reflects the number of hours worked in excess of those required to produce labour's subsistence. This excess represents surplus value (S), while the necessary hours constitute variable capital (V); therefore the rate of surplus value is $\frac{S}{V}$. A rise in *relative* surplus value results from a fall in V, the number of hours required to maintain workers at a constant level of subsistence. A rise in *absolute* surplus value occurs when S increases due to lengthening the working day. The rate of surplus value shows the extent to which capitalists force workers to produce beyond the amount paid in wages, which Marx defines as the degree of capitalist exploitation; the higher is $\frac{S}{V}$, the greater is the share of output taken by capitalists.

The size of $\frac{S}{V}$ depends upon:

(i) the length of the working day. Some notion of a 'normal day' emerges from capitalist-worker negotiations, and increasing the hours worked is the major method of extending exploitation where production is labour intensive. Such a strategy faces physical limits set by health considerations, against which capital pushed during early industrialisation until it met worker resistance through trade union activity and legislation.

(ii) the intensity of the labour process. Exploitation may be increased by extracting greater effort in the same time, for example by speeding up the pace of work, by mechanisation and by having a greater number of machines for each worker to supervise.

(iii) the proportion of the working day required for workers to produce the value of their labour power, *i.e.* necessary labour time. The rate of surplus value rises if technical progress reduces necessary labour time.

(iv) the productivity of labour. If labour's productivity rises, while hours and intensity of work remain unchanged, the rate of surplus value increases.

To explain the existence of exploitation under capitalism Marx draws a distinction between labour and labour power. *Labour* is the source of value and can no more possess a specific value than heat can have a particular temperature. It is an activity not a commodity. On the other hand, *labour power*, the capacity to create value, is a commodity whose value like that of all others is determined by the labour time socially necessary for its production. The human attributes of each worker constitute a stock of potential labour power which commands a wage proportional to the hours needed to produce it. These comprise the time it takes to rear, feed, clothe and house workers, and to maintain their children.

When capitalists acquire a stock of potential labour power, they can compel their employees to work longer and more intensely than is necessary to reproduce this stock. Therefore they exact more hours of labour than they pay for. Since commodities sell at a price proportional to the hours that enter into their production, a difference emerges between the value of output and of labour power, which accrues to capitalists through the mechanics of market operation. By appropriating surplus value, capital exploits labour, although it pays workers the full value of their labour power and receives from consumers the full value of the commodity it sells. The volume of profits depends upon the excess of output per unit of labour over the consumption necessary for that output.

Marx argues that labour power possesses the unique characteristic of adding to the product a value greater than its own. Profit originates from unpaid labour and such exploitation allows capitalists to enjoy unearned income, because they provide no equivalent in exchange for the commodities they receive. The operation of labour markets enables them to appropriate surplus value, given that workers own only labour power while capitalists possess means of production. Capitalism cannot exist without exploitation; if surplus value permanently fell to zero, capitalists would no longer command the resources that enable them to control the labour process.

Once labour power becomes a commodity, the unique ability of labour to confer value is sufficient to explain both production of the surplus and its appropriation by capitalists, without recourse to theories of unequal exchange. Since all products exchange at their transformed values, profit is created in production where exploitation occurs. When capitalists and workers conclude a bargain, both use the commodities exchanged; workers consume wage goods, while capitalists compel surplus labour. New commodities emerge, whose value includes a surplus value belonging to the capitalist, yet simultaneously workers maintain their labour power which they resell to obtain a livelihood. Capitalist relations are thus reproduced by a continuous process, in which capital appropriates part of the value created by labour.

Marx argues that workers obtain the value of their labour power, making no appeal to robbery, unfair pricing and restriction of production nor claiming that workers must in their weakness accept any terms imposed. These phenomena constitute additional rather than basic sources of exploitation. Marx did not rely on market imperfections to generate exploitation; he explains its existence under perfect competition, however empirically significant frictions might be. A class monopoly of ownership of the means of production is consistent with perfect competition among individual firms. Competitive exchange of labour power hides a class relation between workers dispossessed of the means of production and capitalists who own them.

Certain objections have been raised to Marx's theory of exploitation:

(i) Marx's analysis rests upon the labour theory of value, so that economists who reject this theory also reject Marx's proof of the existence of capitalist exploitation.

(ii) Schumpeter (1942) argued that, even if the labour theory of value is valid for other commodities, it cannot be applied to labour since this procedure implies that people are produced on the basis of financial calculation. As they are not, it cannot be assumed that the value of labour power is proportional to the hours that enter into its production. However, this objection fails to distinguish between labour and labour power. Labour as the source of value is an activity not a commodity and is the outcome of human relations, not produced according to the costs incurred. It is not people but labour power that is consumed and reproduced in the process of production according to the rationality of profit maximisation.

(iii) Marx's theory of surplus value is untenable on its own assumptions if applied to a stationary process. A perfectly competitive equilibrium is impossible to maintain if capitalists enjoy exploitation gains, since each would attempt to expand output in order to make greater profits. The ultimate effect is to increase the demand for labour and raise wages at the expense of surplus value until exploitation profits are eliminated. This criticism is not decisive when two additional considerations are introduced:

(a) Perfect competition is unlikely to occur in actuality, so that economies of scale, institutionsl frictions and credit problems may permit exploitation profits to persist at long run equilibrium.

(b) Marx is less concerned with the stationary equilibrium which capitalism is unlikely to attain than with the dynamics of transformation in economic structures. Surplus value may be impossible to achieve at perfectly competitive equilibrium, yet be ever present because equilibrium is never established. Exploitation gains may tend to vanish without doing so in practice because they are continually recreated by the invention of new products and processes of production.

(iv) Marx accepts that the cost of reproducing labour power contains a cultural element in excess of subsistence, which provides the various forms of consumption that induce workers to accept their lot. However, he is vague about how the volume of such luxuries is determined, but implies that custom is crucial. The past level of real wages may be decisive in forming present expectations, but the logical dilemma of the determination of the original standard remains unresolved. Consequently defining the cultural element in the cost of reproducing labour power is extremely difficult. If the definition is sufficiently wide to embrace all workers' consumption it becomes a trivial tautology, but attempts at setting limitations lack a logically coherent basis.

(v) The theory of surplus value basically argues that capitalists appropriate part of the product without contributing to it, *i.e.* profits are unearned income. Controversy on this point is central to the debate about Marxism, but is rarely raised explicitly. Orthodox economists regard profit as the reward for abstinence from consumption and for risk taking. However, these functions command a reward because the wherewithal to wait and take risks is a scarce one that workers do not possess. In one sense this consideration justifies profit, because positive net investment is possible only if some individuals postpone consumption and receive a reward for doing so; profits are both the incentive for, and the source of, capital accumulation. But this defence of profit rests upon the assumption of privately-owned means of production, which it in to way justifies. Ultimately all theories of profit rest on the institutional fact that workers own few, if any, non-human productive resources. Therefore the debate between Marxists and non-Marxists focusses on the crucial issue of whether private property in productive equipment, with the inequality it inherently entails, can be justified.

Recognition of these problems does not obscure the insights yielded by Marx's theory. It at least provides a precise meaning for the emotive concept of exploitation. More significantly, the surplus value concept identifies one of the central processes of capitalism — its tendency to channel the surplus towards capitalists for investment. Profits arise not because individuals abstain from luxury spending but because most of the working population produces more than it consumes. Such a gap is necessary for economic growth in any society, but under capitalism a minority class owns it and controls its use.

The theory of surplus value clarifies the relationship between capital and labour by demonstrating that, when the product is distributed, the crucial division is of labour time. The hierarchical character of the labour process is essential to maximise surplus value; the worker sells, and the capitalist buys, not an agreed amount of labour, but the potential to labour over a specific period which capitalists attempt to realise. Consequently the labour process contains a coercive element embodied in a code of industrial discipline, which employers impose upon employees in an endeavour to maximise output from the labour power which they have purchased. Through the production of surplus value, workers consolidate the power that exploits them, and perpetuate inequality. Marx's theory stresses that the key to analysis of any productive process which generates a surplus is the institutional datum of who owns and controls it. Exploitation occurs when one class possesses the means of production, thereby being able to appropriate the product of surplus labour.

CAPITAL ACCUMULATION

The working class produces an output of which it receives only a part, in the form of consumption goods. Capitalists claim the remainder as profit, which can be put to three alternative uses — saving, consumption or accumulation. Marx argues that most surplus value is inevitably used for accumulation, *i.e.* to create additional means of production, for two interrelated reasons:

(i) Capitalist psychology, manifested as 'the historical

mission of the bourgeoisie', tends to abstinence from hedonistic enjoyment in order to expand productive forces, so laying the basis for future abundance. Marx did not rely on this explanation but sought a compulsion sufficiently powerful to account for psychological motivations.

(ii) More significantly, capitalism can never be stationary, as it is continuously revolutionised from within by the creation of new products and new techniques which threaten the viability of existing business methods. Consequently firms are compelled to accumulate to safeguard their position. Individual capitalists face three imperatives: one, to make a profit in order to maintain their integrity — two, to guarantee future profits. For this, the most effective technology is required — three, to use this technology efficiently often involves new machinery and revised production methods. Competition thus imposes the necessity for accumulation; if one business firm consumes or saves all its profits productive equipment becomes less modern, so that its commodities embody more labour time than is socially necessary. The workforce expends the same labour time as before but produces less value. Surplus value declines and the capitalist's viability is threatened.

By compelling accumulation capitalism secures rapid economic growth. Firms are dominated by the uncertainty arising from competition and the lack of overall regulation, which impels a continuous search for profit and therefore maximum accumulation. An increasing proportion of the population is forced to sell its labour power to obtain a livelihood, placing itself under the authority of capitalists. Two related processes contribute to accumulation — the use of surplus value as additional capital and the spread of capitalist relations.

These relations need to be maintained, *i.e.* after each period of production there must exist those willing and able to re-sell their labour power and capitalists willing and able to buy it. Workers remain *able* to sell their labour power, because they are paid a wage high enough to ensure continued fitness to produce, while making good wear and tear suffered during employment. Workers remain *willing* to re-sell their labour power because their exclusion from ownership of the means of production precludes any other possibility of obtaining an income. Capitalists are *able* to hire workers out of the resources they command from past output, while they are *willing* to employ because they make a profit by selling the commodities that workers produce for more than their cost.

The theory of accumulation clarifies the character of exploitation; the working class exchanges its labour power against its own past labour. By appropriating the products of stored-up labour, capitalists exercise authority in the current labour process because they use profits from previous production to acquire machinery and plant. Workers' own past activity confronts them as capital, an alien power. The threat of actual or potential competition provides the incentive to accumulate, so that Marx's overall picture of capitalism is of an economic system with an inner compulsion to expand production and raise productivity, yet ruled by certain laws inherent in its social base that ultimately limit its growth.

THE TREND TOWARDS MONOPOLY

Marx visualises accumulation as a process compelled by competition. Given the existence of economies of large-scale production and the implicit Marxist assumption that the amount of capital employed by individual businesses is governed by their own accumulation, each attempts to increase its size by re-investing profits. Since not all enterprises are equally efficient, production becomes increasingly concentrated among the more successful. Competition is waged by cutting unit costs, which depend crucially upon the scale of production, so that larger capitalists tend to drive the smaller out of business. This process is accelerated by the growth of financial institutions possessing vast quantities of investible funds.

Initially concentration proceeds at the level of individual firms through their re-investment of profits to improve productive techniques. Greater division of labour, and automation, brings a separation of processes within the factory and the need for larger establishments. The capital required for optimal efficiency increases, so that scope for independent activity by small capitalists narrows. Subsequently firms aggregate to form joint stock companies, while those retaining a separate identity attempt to establish restrictive practices. Multinational corporations which divide global markets among themselves represent the latest concentration of capital.

Competitive capitalism thus undermines its own existence by laying the basis for some degree of monopoly power, *i.e.* the ability to influence appreciably the supply and price of a commodity. Monopolies seek to maximise profit by raising prices and restricting output. Firms continue as rivals but price competition is largely replaced by sales campaigns founded upon product differentiation. Technical progress raises the minimum scale of investment required for industrial efficiency, so that small and medium-sized businesses are progressively excluded for lack of sufficient finance. The challenge of new competitors is lessened as industrial entry is limited to those possessing large initial stocks of capital. This phenomenon constitutes the foundation of monopoly capitalism. Ultimately even the largest enterprises are unable to provide the required investment, so that the state becomes obliged to supply funds, creating a contradiction between private ownership and the public mobilisation of finance.

During the initial stages of industrialisation, the size of capitalist firms was limited by both the availability of capital and the management capacities of their owners. These limits can be overcome by modern joint-stock corporations, which enable aggregates of wealth to be assembled that transcend the total wealth of those working in the enterprise, while vesting operational control in specialised managerial staff. The trend to monopoly changes the composition of the middle class as the self-employed become transformed into sellers of labour power; simultaneously capital accumulation promotes a new stratum between foremen and managers, consisting of engineers, technicians, and research, sales and publicity staff.

Marx's theory of concentration focusses exclusively on the size of individual capitals, while its analysis of outcomes is hampered by an apparatus which cannot deal effectively with oligopoly. However, its contributions remain substantial:

(i) To predict the advent of big business in Marx's time, when industrial models derived from the competitive Lancashire cotton trade, was in itself a great achievement.

(ii) Marx's concept of increasing concentration is vindicated by the subsequent development of imperfect competition theories, although these remain an uneasy amalgam of total and zero control situations suggesting the need for a new analytical structure divorced from exclusive concentration on the price and quantity facets of market power, exemplified by Holland's (1975) attempt at a model of meso-economic power, *i.e.* a new mode of production that divorces macro policy from micro structure. The trend to monopoly creates market structures in which producers are neither pure price takers nor price makers, but the decisions of a few in aggregate determine business parameters.

(iii) The experience of more than a century supports Marx's prediction, in that a small number of large enterprises command an increasing proportion of output, employment and investment. In Britain the hundred largest firms increased their share of net output from 15% in 1910 to 20% in 1950 to 46% in 1970 and to 66% in 1980. The largest twenty firms now account for a third of total capital employed and the largest hundred for three-fifths. Furthermore the phenomenon of interlocking directorships based on extensive interpretation between industrial and finance capital means that monopoly power exceeds that suggested by industry concentration ratios. The National Institute of Economic and Social Research estimates that by the turn of the century twenty-one companies will control three-quarters of the non-nationalised sector of British manufacturing.

Similar trends have occurred in the financial and credit systems. Four of the private clearing banks (Barclays, Lloyds, Midland and National Westminster) account for 90% of total current and deposit accounts. Six firms possess one half of hire purchase business and three of these are controlled by the four biggest banks. 47% of life funds belong to the largest four companies in the British life assurance industry, while the four largest non-life insurance firms account for 60% of premium income. Moreover, twelve companies feature in the top twenty-five in both types of insurance.

(iv) Marx relates concentration to accumulation, so that the former is not only empirically related to the latter but is also part of its logic. Therefore the formation of industrial conglomerates and the social situation they create become inevitable.

The trend to monopoly implies a concentration of power, as it tends to create closer collaboration between political and business interests. The state expresses the interests not merely of the capitalist class but of the dominant monopoly groups within it.

THE FALLING RATE OF PROFIT

Marx shares the opinion of most classical economists that the rate of profit shows a long-run tendency to decline, although few sought to substantiate their a priori views by empiracal data. He stresses three factors tending to reduce the average rate of profit (under-consumption, disproportionality and rising organic composition of capital), each elaborated by later Marxists.

(A) Under-Consumption

Under-consumption derives from a lack of effective demand, which prevents capitalists from realising profits. Wages fulfill a dual role as both costs and purchasing power, so that capitalists face a contradiction whereby they endeavour to cut costs at the risk of reducing demand for their products. These difficulties of realisation imply that firms require minimum labour costs for themselves but high wages to generate sales over the rest of the economy. When demand falls the first impact is usually upon profits, to which capitalists react by reducing expenses. They can only cut back on fixed capital if they can obtain purchasers, which is unlikely during a slump. Therefore wages and jobs tend to fall, which further reduces consumption and reinforces the downward spiral of depression with a falling trend in incomes, output and employment. Keynes (1936) argued that state manipulation of aggregate demand through fiscal and monetary techniques could prevent crises of realisation, but experience since 1945 suggests that this policy may create other problems such as inflation. More fundamentally, the rise in labour's share of national income which has occurred in most western economies during the twentieth century[2] makes it difficult to argue that under-consumption is a major cause of any decline in the rate of profit.

Consequently some modern Marxists, notably Glyn and Sutcliffe (1972), reverse Marx's arguments by asserting that a rising labour share with consequent over-consumption causes a falling rate of profit. They believe that shrinking profits from the mid-1960s were due to a combination of intensified international competition and greater trade union bargaining power. Union strength increased *quantitatively* as the degree of unionisation in Britain rose each year from 1967 to become over 50% of the workforce for the first time in 1974, and *qualitatively* with the maintenance of full employment between 1940 and 1970 which enabled workers to intensify wage claims due to receding fears of job insecurity. Simultaneously, fiercer international competition prevented capital from passing on all increases in labour costs in the form of higher prices to consumers.

But the Glyn and Sutcliffe hypothesis faces certain difficulties. Britain's experience is not easily generalised to other advanced capitalist economies, because it suffered a unique low growth syndrome which generated self-reinforcing, depressive effects on investment and profitability. Moreover, declared profits may not be synonymous with those actually enjoyed; multinational corporations today account for over half of the United Kingdom's manufacturing output and they can easily understate their income by transfer-pricing profits to overseas tax havens.[3] Recent declines in profit are due to underemployment of capital during a recession; thus declared profits rose in the early 1970s reflation, but fell back under subsequent government attempts to depress demand. Nor do Glyn and Sutcliffe consider the different impact of union wage push on large and small firms. Union pressure to generalise the wage increases gained from large oligopolistic corporations might squeeze smaller firms' profits and reinforce the unequal competition between them. Intensified industrial concentration, and pressure for government aid to capital, could result.

(B) Disproportionality

Capitalist development is essentially unplanned, as no firm can individually control all the parameters it faces nor ever obtain perfect information about them. Corporate planning is inevitably based on partial influence and knowledge. Furthermore, even large companies are compelled to concentrate almost entirely on the factors affecting their own balance sheets, although the consequences of corporate decisions become, with the trend to monopoly, more far-reaching. A contradiction emerges within the capitalist mode of production; firms take decisions on the basis of phenomena local to them, but the impact of their decisions becomes increasingly global. Disproportionality results, *i.e.* imbalances between the production plans of different sectors due to uncoordinated development. Incongruity between investment and consumption goods industries is particularly likely to occur. Disproportionality, involving contradictions between the plans of different firms, tends to exert downward pressure on the rate of profit.

Excess productive capacity often emerges from competitive, capital accumulation. Consequently funds are attracted towards alternative investment outlets such as industries characterised by small establishments and easy entry. Ultimately competition intensifies and the rate of profit becomes depressed. A further possibility is the export of capital, especially to developing countries with abundant raw materials, cheap and plentiful labour, and high profitability. Such 'imperialism' is common to dominant capitalist nations; twentieth-century U.S.A., like nineteenth-century Britain, accumulates capital in developing countries' export industries—*e.g.* the recent oil investments.

Disproportionality can take a variety of other forms, for example between the public and the private sector, which invest on different criteria, between manufacturing and services, and between regions. Major distortions in any of these spheres can lead to a spiral of decline and a consequent fall in profitability. The concentration of investors on short-term financial gains exacerbates these dangers; thus lucrative speculation in property development can take precedence over accumulation in manufacturing companies, with the long-run outcome of an under-development of manufacturing on which high profits in services ultimately depend.

Such problems are intensified by the fact that technical progress is staggered over time and varies in speed across different industries. Subsequent multiplier and accelerator effects heighten the difficulties of coordination. Government purchasing and financial support provides one method of compensating for the disproportion between large initial outlays on research, development and re-equipment and the long gestation period before profits accrue. Investment incentives, tax allowances and long-term state contracts maintain profits or sustain demand. Such measures mainly benefit large corporations, so that they indirectly reinforce the disproportionality between large and small firms. Moreover, government spending in general can create an imbalance in the size of the public, compared to the private, sector, while particular items (*e.g.* defence expenditure) may accentuate growth among advanced technology industries without reversing decline in other sectors. Therefore state activity to offset disproportionality often involves its own contradictions.

(C) Rising Organic Composition of Capital

Marx argues that competition ensures the use of surplus value to accelerate accumulation, which improves both the quality and the quantity of the capital stock. *The organic composition of capital*, $\frac{C}{V}$ rises, *i.e.* more fixed capital is used in production relative to wages. Empirically the trend in agricultureal, extractive and manufacturing industries has been towards greater capital intensity as simple tasks have been replaced by expensive interrelated machine systems. The value of labour embodied in means of production (C) increases in proportion to that created by living labour (V + S), so that *the rate of profit* $\frac{S}{C+V}$, although equalised through competition, must fall unless the rate of surplus value $\frac{S}{V}$ rises sufficiently rapidly to offset the increase in C. However, a constraint upon the rate of surplus value exists as V shrinks in relation to S; at the extreme, when V becomes a negligible proportion of V + S, S cannot increase faster than V + S. If C grows more rapidly than V + S, the rate of profit inevitably falls in the long run.[4] Marx argues that with increasing mechanisation the organic composition of capital rises, so that if exploitation remains constant, the rate of profit falls. Given that accumulation is inherent to capitalism, the rate of profit tends to decline over time, particularly given the likelihood of under-consumption and disproportionality occurring. But this trend is not inevitable, and Marx suggests the possibility of counteracting tendencies:

(i) Technical progress may cheapen the production of machinery, so that the value of means of production falls relative to that of living labour power. Although more machines are in use, their value (*i.e.* the labour time needed to produce them) is less; the aggregate value of capital increases or declines depending on whether the elasticity of demand for machinery is elastic or inelastic. Consequently no inevitable tendency for C to rise relative to V + S exists. For instance, improved chemical and transportation techniques can reduce stocks at each stage of production and marketing, so that a rise in labour productivity may not be associated with an increase in the organic composition of capital.

(ii) Technical progress raises either the relative surplus value produced by each worker in a given time, due to higher productivity, or the absolute surplus value by increasing the intensity of work. Both influences offset the tendency of the rate of profit to fall.

(iii) The invention of new products and processes may create new opportunities to secure profit. Railway development provides a historical example, reflected in the current American belief that 'capitalism will recover from its present plight when the average family owns a helicopter'. The nature of innovation has changed; when Marx was writing, most technical progress generated similar commodities more cheaply rather than new ones, *i.e.* process rather than product innovations. However, the latter provide the key to sustaining capitalist expansion although often at an uneven rate.

(iv) A fall in profitability is checked when the capitalist mode of production extends into new spheres of activity or overseas markets with a lower organic composition of capital. Nineteenth-century foreign trade cheapened raw material and food costs so increasing the rate of profit. The scope for such a strategy becomes much less as capitalist relations predominate; indeed it operates in reverse when competition from developing countries compels an increase in accumulation, and thus the organic composition of capital, in advanced economies.

(v) The ability of multinational corporations to transfer price profits to their subsidiaries in low tax havens may offset a decline in the rate of profit.

(vi) The relative scarcity of capital is maintained if new demands upon productive capacity can be created. A crucial commercial function is to stimulate novel wants, as exemplified by the post-1945 expansion in the resources devoted to advertising and public relations.

(vii) The state may introduce policies designed to offset the falling rate of profit, such as wage restraint to raise profit margins, underwriting profits in advanced technology sectors, provision of funds for investment, financing part of the costs of education and training, the supply of cheap fuels and materials from nationalised industries, and the maintenance of aggregate demand.

Marx's theory of the falling rate of profit is logically consistent, given its assumptions that accumulation increases the organic composition of capital and that the rate of exploitation remains constant. The crucial issues are the accuracy of the assumptions and the empirical strength of the countervailing forces, which determine whether the rate of profit declines or increases with capitalist development. The notion of the *inevitability* of the falling rate of profit can be salvaged only if accumulation proceeds within a given state of technology, but such a framework is alien to the dynamic basis of Marxism. Moreover, the absolute mass of surplus value grows as the capitalist mode of production extends, capital accumulates and the number of wage earners grows. These circumstances could reconcile individual capitalists to a fall in the rate of profit. However, theories of the relative strength of the two sets of conflicting influences upon movements in the rate of profit remain controversial.[5] Certainly belief in its inevitable decline rests on a problematic foundation.

THE INDUSTRIAL RESERVE ARMY OF LABOUR

Marx provides an analysis of unemployment distinct from that of orthodox economists. He sees it not as the result of some malfunctioning in the economic system but as an industrial reserve army of labour (*i.e.* a surplus of workers available, and needing to sell their labour power to the capitalist class) necessary for the profitable functioning of capitalism. The reserve army is not merely composed of the registered unemployed but of all available sources of labour such as housewives engaged in wage work, immigrants from poorer countries, part-time, sporadic and home workers. Whenever profitability declines, capital accumulation slows down while unemployment increases due to the cumulative decline in demand for labour. The slump in production, with a consequent rise in the total jobless, provides a mechanism whereby profitability can be restored. First, it drives the less efficient firms out of busines, reducing competition and strengthening the market position of those who survive. Second, it weakens the bargaining power of labour as jobs become increasingly scarce and trade unions less effective.

Therefore unemployment is not an adventitious blemish upon a capitalist economy, but plays a crucial role in maintaining its profitability. Workers' acceptance of the discipline imposed in large-scale production ultimately rests on their lack of an alternative. A failure to accept leads to dismissal, possible difficulty in obtaining another job and in any case all new jobs are subject to similar types of discipline. Factory organisation relies upon capitalists possessing a potential alternative labour supply; should the reserve army become depleted, discipline tends to break down and capitalists face difficulties in maintaining control of the labour process and the distribution of the product.

Surplus value provides the wherewithal for additional means of production, thus playing a crucial role in capital accumulation. The industrial reserve army ensures that surplus value continues to be created, because it prevents wages from being raised sufficiently to eliminate exploitation by placing workers at a permanent bargaining disadvantage. Consequently it helps to sustain capitalism, by reproducing both capitalists who own the means of production and workers who possess only their labour power. Continuous full employment undermines factory discipline and threatens economic stability. Profits rise when aggregate demand is sufficient to maintain full employment, but 'out of control' workers challenge the profit-generating mechanism itself, a more important consideration than a simple comparison of the rates of profit prevailing under different conditions. Thus full employment initially boosts, but ultimately damages, profitability by enabling workers to struggle successfully for higher wages and more control over their job environment.

Marx distinguishes three components of the reserve army of labour — the floating, the latent and the stagnant. The *floating* occurs in centres of industry as workers move from job to job being hired and fired in accord with changes in demand. Unemployment occurs in the process of transfer. With increasing mechnisation this stratum encompasses a larger proportion of the potential workforce. The *latent* reserve army arises in rural areas of industrial capitalist economies, where few job opportunities exist for those released from agriculture by technical progress who tend to move to the cities. In the most developed countries, such as Britain and the United States, this latent pool is largely absorbed. New sources have been uncovered in developing countries, from where immigrants have been received since 1945 at a speed consistent with the requirements of accumulation. Employment of the *stagnant* industrial reserve army of labour is irregular, casual and marginal. It furnishes to capital 'a reservoir of disposable labour power. Its conditions of life sink below the average normal level of the working class; this makes it at once a broad basis of special branches of capitalist exploitation'.[6]

Marx argues that the introduction of labour-saving technology continually replenishes the industrial reserve army. Pressure on labour supplies, and hence falling profits, provides the stimulus for firms to substitute capital for labour in the productive process. Competition generates a further impetus to introduce new production techniques rapidly. When technical progress exhibits a major capital-using bias, a higher flow of gross investment is required to maintain a constant long-run level of employment. If sufficient investment is not forthcoming, an industrial reserve army is created. Thus accumulation tends to reduce labour per unit of output by the restructuring of capital and mechanisation; as capital expands, it destroys other modes of production and releases labour for deployment under capitalist relations.

In the initial stages of industrial capitalism the reserve army rises with the destruction of old crafts and the displacement of artisans by factory production. Moreover, the pool of labour power increases as skill requirements become less; thus women and children frequently replace men in the productive process. When primary accumulation is completed in most sectors, the reserve army is replenished by the constant introduction of new techniques with a labour-saving bias. Any reduction in unemployment tends to increase wages at the expense of profits, so that capitalists attempt to produce the same or greater output with fewer workers. Thus the reserve army tends to rise again.

Marx's theory emphasises that capitalist accumulation is not a steady expansion but a fluctuating process involving acquisition, merger, bankruptcy and unemployment. Whether its major prediction is relevant to contemporary capitalism[7] depends upon the effect of accumulation on the marginal product of labour. If the marginal as well as the average product of labour increases with technical progress, the result is higher output, real wages and employment opportunities. Technological pessimism, of which Marx is an exponent, rests on the fear that experience of rising marginal labour productivity, common to most innovations by the third quarter of the nineteenth century, will not continue. Extremely labour-saving innovations would lower the marginal product of all but the initial workers employed and reduce marginal productivity at the existing level of employment, so that the number of jobs and/or the real wage will fall. Because the limit to output under capitalism is set by the profitable usage of capital equipment rather than by the full employment of labour, there is no theoretical guarantee against this outcome but equally there can be no certainty that it will in practice occur.

Experience over the century since Marx wrote has confirmed the accuracy of his expectation that capital substitutes for labour in agriculture, extraction and manufacturing. However, the aggregate Capital-Output ratio has not risen dramatically due to the growth of employment in private and public services, the majority of which (transport constitutes an exception) are labour intensive. Most of these service jobs have proved difficult to replace by capital-using innovations. This shifting distribution of employment may be halted in future by changes in the character of technical progress. Historically the discoveries exerting major industrial impact, from the steam engine to splitting the atom, essentially found new methods of using energy. Since the computer, the weight of scientific advance has altered towards processing information so that the number of workers required to collect and disseminate data is reduced. The impact of these productivity increases could be a substantial loss in jobs. The production of many items previously depending on mechanical moving parts, *e.g.* watches, cash registers and telephone equipment, has also been revolutionised by new technology; the workforce engaged in producing cash registers halved in both the U.K. and the U.S. as electronic machines replaced mechnical ones, while in retail distribution the computerised point of sale system that carries out stock control as well as computing the prices of goods purchased is transforming techniques. The most substantial employment implications come from the automation of office work made possible by such machines as word processors, which could drastically reduce job opportunities for women workers 40% of whom are currently engaged in clerical jobs.

While the employment of specific groups is at risk because of labour-saving innovation, it is uncertain how many job losses will arise from this source. Barron and Curnow (1979) estimated that 16% of the U.K. workforce, four million people, will be displaced by new technology over fifteen years. Such estimates depend crucially upon such influences as market conditions, capitalist strategy, government policy, and the education and training of the labour displaced. However, it remains a strong possibility that technical progress in the immediate future could undermine the role of services in providing a refuge for the industrial reserve army of labour. Should this occur, Marx's prognostications will carry greater relevance in the future.

THE IMMISERATION OF THE PROLETARIAT

Marx undoubtedly holds that over the course of time real wages, and hence living standards, would fall for better-paid workers and fail to improve in the worst-paid strata, not through transitory circumstances but by virtue of the inherent logic of capitalism's operation. He wrote: 'Along with the constantly diminishing number of the magnitudes of capital ... grows the mass of misery, exploitation, slavery, degradation and oppression'.[8] Marx clearly formulates the theory of absolute impoverishment, *i.e.* that poverty grows with capitalist development. He argues that any rise in real wages is temporary because it sets in motion adaptive capitalist strategies such as compensatory price increases, cuts in investment, rationalisation and replacement of labour by machinery, which create unemployment and stimulate downward pressure on real wages. Mechanisation reduces the demand for skills and causes a deterioration in working conditions, while wages fail to rise with productivity.

For Marx, the industrial reserve army of labour determines real wages, so that living standards fall with capitalist evolution due to rising unemployment. Fluctuations around this trend depend upon temporary expansions or contractions in the reserve army. Marx stresses the ability of trade unions to 'destroy or weaken the ruinous effects of the natural law of capitalist production on their class', but believes that workers' bargaining power remains less than that of capitalists. The tendency for the supply of labour to exceed demand prevents wages from rising above the minimum necessary to enable employees to perform their jobs. These assertions appear to contradict Marx's own model in which the cost of reproducing labour power determines wages, so establishing *an absolute* limit to the degree of exploitation. However, wages can be driven below the long-run cost of reproduction with the consequence of a shrinking labour force. If the trend towards monopoly and an increasing organic composition of capital generate a decline in labour demand, such a shrinkage need not create a shortage of workers and a reversal of the decline in wages.

Moreover, Marx suggests that a traditional and cultural element subject to historical change enters into the normal value of labour power. This element can be equated with the price of those luxuries which experience has incorporated into working-class living standards. Its size depends upon average productivity over the recent past, but a secular increase in the industrial reserve army exerts a downward pressure on real wages, which in the long run reduces the traditional and cultural element in the cost of reproducing labour power by lowering the volume of luxury consumption that the average worker expects. Thus the progressive immiseration of the proletariat proceeds.

Marx's prediction of immiseration was compatible with the observable facts of his period. The behaviour of real wages in Britain during the first half of the nineteenth century is still debated, while the social costs of the industrial revolution bore heavily upon the working class and led to a qualitative deterioration in its environment. Subsequently, however, British average real wages climbed to a level that was 84% higher in 1900 than in 1850. During the twentieth century real wages have continued on an unsteady but secularly upward trend.

Marx underestimates the extent to which real wages can rise under capitalism. The issue is empirical; if capital is measured in terms of labour units, real wages must rise if technical progress produces cheaper wage goods or greater output per hour, provided that the labour force does not grow faster than gross product. Marxists are embarrassed by the falsity of Marx's prognosis, and various attempts to salvage his model have been devised:

(i) Some assay the impossible task of showing that material living standards have fallen since 1850.

(ii) Others claim that Marx's theory applies not to absolute, but to relative, labour income, *i.e.* the proportion of national output accruing to labour. Whether or not this interpretation of Marx is correct, the behaviour of relative shares is inconsistent with the prediction. In Britain the wage share has remained remarkably constant since 1870, while that of total labour income rose.[2] During the twentieth century increases of varying magnitude in the same direction occurred in other advanced capitalist economies.

(iii) Some argue that non-material standards of living have fallen so that deterioration in the quality of life has offset the increase in real wages. Marx includes within immiseration the loss of status and craft pride, insecurity and alienation that capitalist development generates. Alienation is an integral feature of industrial capitalism's operation yet is unlikely to have increased sufficiently to outweigh the financial improvement in working-class living standards. The alienation involved in modern production is substantial (*e.g.* assembly lines), but a golden age free from alienation never existed. Nineteenth-century labour was heavily alienated.

(iv) It can be argued that the tendency for real wages to fall is inherent to capitalism, but that exceptional conditions since 1850 have prevented the operation of this law, so providing a closed season for capitalism. A number of candidates for this role have been proposed:

(a) Late nineteenth-century Marxists pointed to the extension of the U.S. frontier and the opening-up of new countries.

(b) It is suggested that colonial expansion enabled imperial capitalists to prevent a fall in their workers' real wages by indirectly offering them a share in the exploitation profits derived from overseas. Such modern Marxists as Sweezy (1972) analyse the unequal structure of centre-periphery relations within the contemporary international economy, which enables exploitation of less developed countries to continue.

(c) Strachey (1956) argued that in the socio-economic conditions of Marx's time the tendency of wages to fall was overwhelming, but this trend can be offset under universal suffrage as this modifies the environment in which employers and workers bargain. The development of effective trade unions and the growth of the Cooperative Society accentuate this process. Strachey believed that the modest redistribution achieved through union and political pressure constituted strong evidence that in the absence of such activity a wage rise below productivity growth would be the probable outcome. Without working-class industrial and political organisation, Marx would have been correct but he failed to foresee the collective forces that originated within capitalism to counter its inherent economic tendencies, with the result that labour's relative share improved modestly while workers' absolute living standards rose. On Strachey's formulation, political changes possess economic consequences, so that a feedback occurs between economics and politics rather than the supremacy of economic influences postulated by Marx. Whatever the merits of such an approach, it is un-Marxist in its implication that the rate of exploitation can be politically determined through a bargaining or legislative process.

Robinson (1942) attempted to modify the theory of immiseration in view of the rise in real wages during the preceding century. She argued that productivity growth places an upper limit on wage increases. Effective trade unions tend to push wages towards this limit, while monopoly power prevents a rise above it. Real wages vary with the fortunes of the class struggle between a lower range loosely set by the cost of reproducing labour power and an upper range set by the rate of profit at which capitalists refuse to reinvest. She believed that the crucial comparison is not with past living standards but between current incomes and their potential level under a different economic system, in which capitalist consumption ceases to exist because it no longer constitutes a necessary cost to induce the supply of capital. From this standpoint Marx's theory of immiseration is not correct in its original version, but remains significant by emphasising how capitalism operates to deprive workers of part of their potential income in the form of capitalist consumption.

ALIENATION

Marx's theory of alienation lies outside the scope of economics as conventionally defined, but it has recently stimulated significant research—for example by Braverman (1974) and Friedman (1977). In Marx's terminology alienation occurs when humanity is unfree; people do not consciously control their conditions of existence, because their own productive powers are independent determinants of their behaviour. Capitalism expands commodity production and creates capital as a dominant power whose requirements constitute the source of exploitation, due to the exclusion of a majority from ownership of the means of production which are fragmented into competing units.

All transactions are reduced to a cash nexus, as each capitalist is compelled to maximise surplus value through exploitation of labour. Human potentialities and aspirations are realisable only by the market acquisition of goods and services, so that social interaction takes place through inanimate quantities. Each person responds to cultural requirements through the medium of commodity prices and quantity of commodities, which are merely manifestations of the capacity to produce; thus producers are controlled by their own collective ability instead of directly determining their environment through conscious regulation. Technical progress either liberates or enslaves, depending on how it is applied and on whose authority. In practice, however, production largely consists of people servicing machinery, and most workers, whose jobs are not intrinsically creative, seek satisfaction in leisure pursuits.

In every mode of production labour and inanimate resources combine to generate output, but the specific manner in which this union is achieved distinguishes different socio-economic formations. Under capitalism they unite via the wage contract whereby workers submit to the control of capitalists or their hired managers during the productive process. Once such contracts are completed labour becomes subordinate in the industrial hierarchy, working with materials to produce commodities it does not own.

Alienation is reflected in the consciousness of capitalist

society. Marx's theory of commodity fetishism analyses the mechanism through which people perceive the economy as operating independently and ruling them in an arbitrary and uncontrollable manner, so failing to appreciate that they are governed by tendencies resulting from the structure of social relations. Moreover, the existence of classes is hidden by the individualisation of market operations. Thus contemporary disquiet over collective action by workers indicates the way such behaviour jars with the dominant ideology of free exchange between individuals. So long as capitalism appears the natural order, individualistic theories seem not only obvious but also, in their essentials, just. The consciousness of the ruling class provides each epoch's central concepts which rationalise its specific interest in universal terms. On this basis Marx is critical of bourgeois freedom (*i.e.* the absence of constraints on individual action) as the highest form of liberty. In contrast he argues that people are free to the extent that they consciously control both nature and their social conditions of existence in accord with their historically developing needs.

All are alienated under capitalism but since its root cause is located in the specific relations of production that determine the organisation of the labour process, alienation is greatest for the proletariat. Workers' humanity is devalued by their subordination to the material objects they produce, which are appropriated by the capitalist, while labour power becomes a commodity whose job environment is beyond its control. The division of labour increases total output by reducing productive tasks to simple operations, but in separating manual from mental work it narrows both.[9] As workers become appendages of machinery, capital dominates labour and stands opposed to it as an autonomous alien power. Employment is not an expression of humanity nor a means of developing the potential for conscious creativity but an activity, frequently degrading or boring, undertaken to obtain a livelihood. Neoclassicals see 'disutility' as a necessary cost of supplying labour power but Marx believes that people require a 'normal portion of work'. Self-realisation is frequently achieved through aims self-posited and obstacles surmounted, *i.e.* labour as freedom contrasted to repulsive labour externally imposed. The need for free time to pursue creativity applies to all and is not the specialised province of minorities. Thus Fromm (1965) argued that workers' alienation springs from lack of control over the products, instruments and conditions of their labour.

Braverman (1974) noted the uncertainty which labour power presents to capitalists because its performance is affected by the subjective feelings of workers. Management seeks to reduce this variability through its control of the labour process; a principal strategy is separating the conception of tasks from their execution, a process which reduces the skill required from most workers. Thus the current organisation of production tends to constrain rather than stimulate creative potentialities; for example, Blackburn and Mann (1979) found that the labour market in Peterborough, not a depressed English town, offered little opportunity to exercise skill.[10] Such deskilling was an unconscious feature of early capitalism, yet became accelerated and systematic with the development of twentieth-century scientific management. The pioneer of this movement, Taylor (1911), argued that management is limited and frustrated whenever labour retains any decision-making powers within the workplace. The first principle of his system is to gather and develop knowledge of labour processes, the second is to concentrate this knowledge as the exclusive property of management, and the third is to use such a monopoly to control the execution of each stage of production.

Under capitalist social relations humanity exists contrary to its potential of being in conscious control of its own activity, so that the abolition of capitalism is a necessary but not a sufficient condition for overcoming alienation. Marx argues that revolutionary action to abolish bourgeois property relationships will arise from the conditions that create alienation, because these also generate class conflict and contradictions within the economy. Capitalism creates the possibility of a free society by developing human capacity to dominate nature through the creation of wealth, so providing a basis for the 'universal development of individuals'. People can only control social relations by knowledge, which develops when they become universal producers. Then the economy ceases to be a mystery confronting individuals as a system of independent forces. Only the proletariat has the power, interest and capability to transform society; it possesses the power because it forms a majority, the interest as its economic and social position deteriorates, and the capability since its own organisations approximate increasingly to those of socialism. Industrial unrest and class struggle spring from deeper roots than financial conflicts, important through these are, for they derive from the straining of humanity to be free. Wage demands often compensate for lives wasted, time lost and freedom alienated. Such unsatisfied impulses promote the development of radical needs.[11]

In addition to the common orthodox response of neglect, a number of objections to Marx's theory of alienation are advanced:

(i) A defence of capitalism can be constructed from the propositions of neoclassical welfare economics, yet these are inapplicable to actual variants of capitalism except on restrictive assumptions that are not empirically plausible or even approximate to reality. Neoclassical analysis rests on three main propositions; it assumes that actors' preferences are exogenous, that actors are rational and that interactions take place in an environment characterised by perfect knowledge.

Belief that preferences are exogenous to the operation of the economy conflicts with sociological research and everyday experience, yet neoclassical welfare theory assesses the efficiency of economic structures in terms of their fulfilment of preferences. Theoretical recognition of the socially endogenous nature of preferences undermines such logic, for efficiency can be evaluated only if the standards of judgement (preference structures) are independent of what is being judged (economic structures). Marx's theory of alienation is not open to this objection.

The second assumption, rationality, is also problematic, partly because it is untrue of important areas of economic activity and partly because the concept itself is tautological (as can be seen if one tries to find a case of someone not attempting to maximise expected utility). Moreover, neoclassical mechanisms of rational orientation are confined to particular behaviour patterns which result in individual exchange. These are not, however, the forms that rational action takes in certain crucial economic spheres. Only by incorporating the specific social relations of capitalism can rationality be analysed when it is neither individualistic nor exchange-orientated, but these relations are data which neoclassical theory neglects. Its consequently limited definition of rationality is unsuitable for studying the actual operation of economies.

The assumption of perfect knowledge is crucial to the neoclassical paradigm; as Blaug (1968) noted, 'its fundamental theorems rest upon the assumption of perfect certainty'. This is ometimes explicitly stated, but usually is left implicit. It is a useful simplification when studying economies which change slowly or are isolated, but is dubious for analysis of a capitalist economy. The basic organisation of capital into a multitude of autonomous competing units creates uncertainty which operates through the expectations of capitalists. Its significance arises when analysing processes which move economies away from equilibrium.

(ii) Such works as Popper (1945) and Berlin (1958) incorporate possible answers to Marx's theory of alienation. Berlin's defence of the negative concept of freedom against the positive definition of Marx is invalid, because it regards ideas as independent forces possessing an autonomous momentum of their own. Therefore they become divorced from the socio-economic structures that provide their historic role and can be manipulated into any causal factor that subjective opinion requires. Pursuit of positive freedom is believed to culminate in totalitarianism, so that bourgeois freedom and its capitalist context are defended by a flimsy negative argument. Popper's similar reasoning encounters the same objections.

(iii) Marx's concept of alienation rests on a view of what humanity has the potential to become which many, *e.g.* Aron (1965), regard as unattainable. Differing views on this topic constitute a crucial value judgement when assessing Marx's theory, but to classify it as insignificant on this ground implies that alienation is a universal aspect of the human condition in industrial societies.[12] To admit otherwise attributes some validity to Marx's critique. Thus Hymer and Roosevelt (1972) argue that, if the market provides a model to justify capitalism on the grounds of its apparent freedom, actual conditions of work furnish its critique (coercion, inequality etc.) as well as clues to an economy enjoying a non-possessive, non-individualistic organisation of production. Lindbeck (1977), denying this point, confuses the social relations specific to capitalist exploitation with technological forces inherent in modern industry. He also confuses authority during productive activity with the coordination of complex processes; both are managerial functions under capitalism, but only the latter necessarily occurs under all modes of production.

Marx's categorisation of social relationships is superior to that of neoclassical theory because it relates to historically specific stages of capitalism, while only limited and unsatisfactory refutations of his concept of alienation have appeared. The concept lends itself to further research on the nature of the production process. The labourer's work is involuntary, so that each day involves a struggle between capital and labour; capitalists attempt to get workers to perform tasks they would not voluntarily choose, and workers try to resist. Marx analyses capitalist production in terms of this conflict, showing the forms of resistance deployed by workers and the pressures exerted by capitalists to maintain control. Orthodox economics hardly touches upon these problems, but their detailed discussion can be found in the literature of corporate organisation, industrial relations, industrial sociology and psychology, where they are usually approached from the standpoint of control. One of the tasks for radicals is to reverse this approach and develop counter-organisation strategies, particularly as the frontier of job control between employers and employees in the workplace is continually shifting under the impact of markets, technology and group power. When workers possess some ability to regulate the labour process, they thwart efforts to realise the full productive potential of their labour power. Management endeavours to undermine such job regulation by asserting its control, not only in a formal sense but by dictating each step of the labour process including standards of performance.

THE TRADE CYCLE

Capitalist development has been uneven over time, yet Marx was the first economist to recognise the existence of the trade cycle rather than analysing crises in isolation. The perception of cyclical oscillations was in itself a major pioneering achievement. Thus Schumpeter (1942) concluded that 'in Marx we find practically all the elements that ever enter into any serious analysis of business cycles.' However, he possesses no simple theory but looks at a range of influences, while stressing the role of accumulation and the reserve army of labour in promoting immiseration. Logically this process could occur at an even rate, but while Marx describes the cycle in detail, he never welds his hypotheses into a coherent explanation of why the underlying contradictions of capitalism manifest themselves in endogenous, periodic cyclical fluctuations. He argues that increasing socialisation of production magnifies the intensity of crises and creates a cycle of wider amplitude. Prior to the final breakdown of capitalism when its evolution disrupts its institutional framework, it operates with heightened difficulty and displays fatal symptoms. Therefore Marx integrates recurrent crises, as the harbingers of eventual collapse, with secular trends. However, without additional hypotheses, the ultimate causes of breakdown cannot be responsible for cyclical fluctuations since the two phenomena may exist separately; at most, periodic depressions contribute to a finally untenable socio-economic situation.

Marx perceives the weaknesses of Say's (1803) law, which held that supply creates its own demand so that a deficiency of aggregate purchasing power can never occur in a world of scarcity. He argues that, while every sale is a purchase, use of money permits a time lag between them, *i.e.* no seller is compelled to purchase immediately. Commodity production and money separate sales from purchases so that crises become possible although not inevitable, arising when there is an imbalance between purchases and sales (*i.e.* some of the revenue derived from sales is not used to buy other commodities but is hoarded). For Marx, the rate of profit, the key motivational variable in a capitalist economy, is a crucial determinant of this imbalance. If capitalists fail to achieve expected profitability, they tend to reduce output; purchases and sales become unbalanced as they seek to hoard rather than employ productive resources. Consequently overproduction, unemployment and slump are not aberrations but frequent occurrences, because commodity production in a monetary economy contains the possibility of crises.

These possibilities become actualised when changes in profitability initiate a slump. Marx emphasises disproportionality, under-consumption and a rising organic composition of capital as influences generating a falling rate of profit, but stresses the volatility of demand for investment goods as a primary initiating factor while the uneven time pattern of depreciation causes considerable fluctuations in expenditure. Therefore the source of crises is located in a disequilibrating process of accumulation. Maldistribution of income creates further problems as workers' consumption is limited by poverty, and capitalists' consumption by the necessity to re-invest. Accumulation is a function of profit expectations which depend upon consumer demand, so a limitation of the latter curbs the long-run output of capital goods. Crises put on trial the existence of capitalism by demonstrating that its social relations restrict production and become a barrier to further developments of the human capacity to transform nature.

During the early stages of capitalism depressions tend to be deep but short-lived, since a fall in real wages due to a rise in the industrial reserve army of labour often induces a swift recovery. As the accumulation of capital progresses, booms and slumps magnify. Crises facilitate major structural changes for expectations of profitability improve when many capitalists are bankrupted and costs lowered. Consequently production is reorganised and new techniques are introduced. Upswings require increasing profits and expanding markets, but these phenomena undermine themselves in the long run, because any rise in the rate of profit leads to a fall in labour's income share while simultaneously productive capacity grows and exceeds purchasing power. Booms collapse from the attempt to maintain former profit levels in the face of an increased capital stock. Conversely, crises restore the conditions for profitability by destroying capital values.

Certain phenomena are essential for the smooth expansion of a capitalist economy: adequate supplies of compliant labour, growing markets, and a balance between different sectors so that no industry constrains the expansion of others and hence of the system as a whole. Crises may result from labour shortage and class struggle, from limited demand, from the emergence of one or more sectors as a bottleneck, or from all simultaneously. The ultimate cause of depression is that capitalism contains no mechanism to ensure that the necessary conditions for continuous expansion are maintained.

A faltering in the rate of profit due to lack of effective demand could originate either in capitalists failing to spend all or part of profits or in workers failing to spend all or part of wages, but in practice the latter is unlikely. Wages are used for maintenance; individual workers save but others borrow, so that for the working class as a whole saving and borrowing are approximately equal and a sharp fall in workers' propensity to consume is improbable. For capitalists the reverse is true; most profits are spent not on personal consumption but are invested in the hope of generating further profit. Therefore capitalists will not spend their incomes unless it appears profitable to do so. Underconsumption, disproportionality and over-accumulation can create the conditions under which non-spending decisions occur. Random shocks are a contiual threat to profits, but a more fundamental problem is the tendency for accumulation to undermine the conditions for profitable production so that capitalists fail to invest because of dissatisfaction with future prospects.

Marx's trade cycle theory has limitations, partly because it is set within the problematic context of a tendency for the rate of profit to fall. No precise location of the upper and lower turning point is provided, while the relationship between under-consumption, disproportionality and a rising organic composition of capital remains unexplored. Moreover, Marx never systematically demonstrates that capitalists are unable to use the state to reduce the amplitude of the cycle. He implies that they will not, but provides no proof that the task is technically impossible nor that it is politically impossible for the capitalist class to initiate or support such policies. Indeed his emphasis on capitalists' rationality, the concentration of capital and the significance of class struggle suggests that the development of state anti-cyclical measure is likely.

Marx adumbrates the most important causes of cyclical fluctuations and in assessing his theory it should be remembered that modern orthodoxy cannot provide a satisfactory explanation of the trade cycle's historical course. This is one of the most complex issues in economic theory, since such crucial variables as investment, profits and expectations are difficult to specify precisely. Moreover, Marx's achievements are impressive, for example his refutation of Say's Law, emphasis on endogeneity and periodicity, the key roles attributed to the rate of profit and deficiency in aggregate demand, the particular volatility of investment and the significance of money as the least uncertain store of value. His theory relates closely to modern neo-Keynesian developments and recent empirical evidence in arguing that instability in the demand for means of production is crucial; investment demand produces a boom, but when it declines, maldistribution prevents a rise in consumption sufficient to absorb the resources previously employed in producing capital goods.

MARX'S ECONOMIC SYSTEM: AN OVERVIEW

'Let us imagine two persons; one who has learned his economics only from the Austrian School, Pareto and Marshall, without ever having seen or even heard a sentence of Marx or his disciples; the other one who, on the contrary, knows his economics exclusively from Marx and the Marxists and does not even suspect that there may have been economists outside the Marxist School. Which of the two will be able to account better for the fundamental tendencies of the evolution of Capitalism? To put the question is to answer it.

But this superiority of Marxian economics is only a partial one. There are some problems before which Marxian economics is quite powerless, while "bourgeois" economics solves them easily. What can Marxian economics say about monopoly prices? What has it to say on the fundamental problems of monetary and credit theory? What apparatus has it to offer for analysing the incidence of a tax or the effect of a certain technical innovation on wages? And (irony of fate!) what can Marxian economics contribute to the problem of the optimum distribution of productive resources in a socialist economy?

Clearly the relative merits of Marxian economics and of modern "bourgeois" economic theory belong to different "ranges". Marxian economics can work the economic evolution of capitalist society into a consistent theory from which its necessity is deduced, while "bourgeois" economists get no further than mere historical description. On the other hand, "bourgeois" economics is able to grasp the phenomena of the every-day life of a capitalist economy in a manner that is far superior to anything the Marxists can produce. Further, the anticipations which can be deduced from the two types of economic theory refer to a different range of time. If people want to anticipate the development of capitalism over a long period a knowledge of Marx is much more effective than a knowledge of Wieser, Bohm-Bawerk, Pareto or even Marshall (though the last named is in this respect much superior). But Marxian economics would be a poor basis for running a central bank or anticipating the effects of a change in the rate of discount' (O. LANGE, 1935).

If ever the whole is more than the sum of the parts, this dictum applies to Marx's economics. He sees class conflict as marking all stages of human society until productive capacity is developed to the point where only the internal operation of capitalism prevents the removal of social struggle. Therefore capitalism destroys its own foundations. Such a dynamic perspective, stressing the fundamental contradiction between socialisation of production and private appropriation in which collective interdependence is harnessed to the search for profit, provides the basis for future threory by looking at economics as a process each stage of which determines the next. It thus occupies a different conceptual world from the comparative statics of orthodox textbooks. Marx considers that capitalism creates conflicting internal forces which ultimately produce a qualitative structural transformation, the key to which lies in the mode of production.

Stored up labour enters into an exchange with living labour on a legally equal footing, but the former is dominant in practice because capitalists possess the power to control society's productive apparatus, which is the creation of past labour appropriated by earlier capitalists and inherited or bought by present ones. Therefore the crystallisation of past labour takes the form of privately owned means of production. Operating in a market economy, these owners must extract a profit from their transactions in order to maintain their position, and the ultimate source of profits is living labour. Marx argues that under capitalism workers build a world that does not belong to them, which includes the entire legal and cultural superstructure controlled by the possessing class.

The property relations of capitalism are crucial to its nature and functioning, with competition between the bourgeoisie compelling accumulation. Capitalism is not some direct expression of a universal economic impulse but a historically concrete form taken by the general need for material production; it exhibits a particular form of rationality in pursuit of unlimited acquisition. It develops humanity's wealth-creating abilities, thereby establishing the precondition for freedom, but its contradictions derive from its organisation as a system of production geared to capital accumulation rather than to consciously meeting needs. Incompatibility between social production and private appropriation arises; the former derives from progressive extension of the division of labour, and the latter from property relations. The development of productive forces is inhibited by the consequences of private ownership, as illustrated in the occurrence of crises of overproduction when resources stand idle despite the existence of unfulfilled needs.

Some of the tendencies prophesied by Marx failed to materialise (*e.g.* the rising organic composition of capital and immiseration), but his essential point that the volume and composition of output is determined by the requirements of capital rather than social needs remains intact. Analysis of capitalism based on its class relations calls into question its existence and poses, if only implicitly, an alternative. Moreover, by taking sociological data and historical developments as the foundation for economic theory, Marx treats social institutions and events of the past as key variables not as exogenous influences in the arguments that generate hypotheses. His concepts of accumulation, concentration and the trade cycle are central contributions to economic thought, while his vision of the economic process as a dynamic sequence rather than as a static allocative mechanism is the framework within which most recent theoretical developments have occurred.

Marx fails to prove conclusively that capitalism necessarily breaks down, since some of the essential transitional stages have not taken place, while even if all materialised breakdown would not be inevitable. Furthermore, the subsequent emergence of socialism constitutes a distinct phenomenon, since other possible consequences of breakdown exist (*e.g.* chaos); certainly, in the event of capitalist collapse, distinct action will be necessary to achieve socialism. Marx does not provide a detailed account of the operation of a socialist economy, but concentrates on the conditions of its emergence, *i.e.* the presence of giant units of industrial enterprise that facilitate socialisation and the emergence of an organised yet exploited proletariat who take control and inaugurate a classless society. Thus the inherent contradictions of capitalism produce its self-destruction, when the expropriators are expropriated and workers take over the accumulated capital.

Marx sees the revolutionary overthrow of capitalism by a class-conscious proletariat as the agency for the realisation of people's humanity. The proletariat's dehumanised condition makes such a solution inevitable; capitalism increases control over nature and forms the working class into an agency whose organisation through trade unions is a harbinger of socialist relations of production (*i.e.* conscious cooperation). Proletarian revolutionary activity constitutes a new form of consciousness which is institutionalised across society under socialism. Capitalism increasingly generates, through the inherent logic of its operation, the social structures and productive power which can only be fully realised in a socialist economy. Marx suggests that the decline of *laissez faire*, the passing of Factory Acts, the emergence of joint stock companies and the development of trade unions were nineteenth-century indicators of this trend, each reflecting a partial awareness of what collective action can achieve.

Therefore Marxism is orientated towards achieving the ideal of human freedom. The gap between what humanity currently is and what it could potentially become is to be bridged by conscious action. Marx's economics contains original and penetrating insights but also some questionable propositions central to his theory of proletarian revolution. Socialist movements remain crucial to humanity's future while contemporary capitalism exhibits internal contradictions which might precipitate its demise, yet Marx's specific model provides only partial guidelines for revolutionary action in the late twentieth century. Modern radicals need to think for themselves and act on their own analysis, if their theory and practice is to possess the required relevance. Nonetheless the usefulness of Marx's general approach and criticisms of capitalism can hardly be over-exaggerated. His stress on the pivotal role of capital accumulation and technical change makes him currently relevant in a way that none of his contemporaries and few of his successors can ever be.

NOTES

1. It is not necessary that people who labour to produce the surplus should also control it. In no past or contemporary society has this been the case; the existence of a surplus provides the opportunity for one class to live off the product of another class's labour. Thus society divides into two groups, the controllers and the producers of the surplus.
2. Burkitt and Bowers (1979) calculated that labour's share of the gross national product in the United Kingdom rose from 55 · 3% between 1910 and 1914 to 78 · 3% in 1976. They also demonstrated that a similar trend took place in other advanced capitalist nations.
3. Holland (1975) discussed transfer pricing in detail.
4. It should be noted that Marx's theory of the falling rate of profit does

not rely on neoclassical explanations, such as the operation of diminishing returns or the initial exploitation of the most profitable investment opportunities. These acquire significance in static rather than dynamic analysis.

5 See, for instance, Howard and King (1975) or Fine and Harris (1979).

6 K. Marx, *Capital*, Vol. 1, p. 602, Moscow: Foreign Language Publishing House, 1961.

7 Marx was certainly correct in the context of his time, because the progression of capitalist, at the expense of pre-capitalist, enterprise released more labourers from the non-capitalist units than could be absorbed into the capitalist sector, owing to the difference in productivity between the two sectors. As long as capitalism grows through a shrinkage of pre-capitalist modes of production, labour supply tends to exceed demand. Eventually demand for labour tends to accelerate beyond supply due to capital accumulation; labour becomes scarce, wages rise at the expense of profits and a crisis develops. Falling profitability slows down the rate of accumulation and reduces the demand for labour at a given accumulation by increasing the organic composition of capital. Therefore the reserve army of labour is eventually recreated.

8 K. Marx, *Capital*, Vol. 1, p. 763, Moscow: Foreign Language Publishing House, 1961.

9 Sohn-Rethel (1978) develops this point.

10 Over 85% of the jobs performed in Peterborough required less skill than their occupant would use in driving a car to work.

11 A concept thoroughly explored by Heller (1974).

12 Thus Lindbeck (1977) argued that problems of industrial disputes and work methods are connected more with technology and large-scale organisation than with the capitalist mode of production.

6 Fabianism

The Fabian Society, formed in 1884, was a small group of intellectuals who became convinced that the power of the state could be acquired peacefully by socialists for the purpose of promoting economic and social reforms that gradually eliminate capitalism. The Fabians did not consciously react to Marx,[1] but their overall philosophy contrasts sharply with the Marxist view of the class nature of capitalist government and the consequent necessity for its revolutionary overthrow. The gains experienced by British workers in the second half of the nineteenth century seemed to undermine this view; the average real wage rose by 40% between 1862 and 1875 while in 1900 it was 33% higher than it had been in 1875. Political advances included universal suffrage for men and the formation of working-class political parties. However, improvements in living standards temporarily ceased during the economic stagnation of the 1880s and 1890s when Booth (1904) and Rowntree (1901) found 40% of the populations of London and York still living in poverty. The development of Fabian philosophy and strategy reflected this background.

Their leading theorist Sydney Webb provided a three-dimensional definition of socialism; *economically*, as the collective administration of interest and rent, leaving to individuals the wages of their labour; *politically*, as the collective ownership of the main instruments of wealth production; and *ethically*, as the recognition of fraternity, the universal obligation of personal service and the subordination of individual ends to the common good. The moral basis of socialism lies in the desire to remove the inequalities caused by private ownership of the means of production and to replace them by some form of classless society. The Fabians argued that progressive taxation of unearned income in combination with a gradual extension of state activity and municipal enterprise provide a non-revolutionary path to socialism, so that in practice they supported almost all government intervention on the ground that it furthered their ultimate purpose. They never considered the possibility that the objectives of state operations should be the criterion for approval.

Their philosophy was a reaction to the prevailing *laissez faire* climate and in order to foster an expansion in the role of governments, they became a research team for social investigation. Nineteenth-century governments, without a modern civil service until the Northcote-Trevellyan reforms of the 1870s took effect, lacked information and policy proposals. The Fabians filled this vacuum and by stressing the need for cooperation to secure improvements became unofficial public servants. The Society's creed of the 'inevitability of gradualness' is crystallised in its motto referring to Fabius Concutator, the Roman general famous for his caution in conducting military operations especially when opposing Hannibal—'Fabius waited most patiently when warring against Hannibal, though many censured his delays; but when the time comes you must strike hard, as Fabius did, or your waiting will be in vain'. This overall philosophy was supported by detailed theories of capitalist exploitation and of the transition to socialism, which provide a coherent socialist alternative to Marxism.

CAPITALIST EXPLOITATION AND THE FABIAN THEORY OF RENT

Socialists need to prove not only that a specific capitalist society is exploitive, but that the best possible arrangement (on bourgeois definitions) retaining private ownership of the means of production inevitably entails exploitation. The utility theory of value pioneered in Britain by Jevons (1871) raises the issue of whether a theory of capitalist exploitation must necessarily rest upon the labour theory of value. Marx attempted to prove that in the capitalist ideal of perfect competition workers are deprived of the full value of their labour by the essential character of productive relations. Such exploitation can only be remedied by a fundamental modification of these relations, so that reform should lead away from, rather than towards, the capitalist optimum. Marx's concept of exploitation was part of a logical system in which the labour theory of value was a central analytical tool. However, in the winter of 1884-5 the Reverend Phillip Wicksteed[2] persuaded the Fabians that the labour theory of value was untenable. He claimed that the development of a different theory based upon utility erodes the basis of Marx's argument and undermines the edifice built upon it.

If the labour theory of value is wrong and the Fabians accepted Wicksteed's argument, socialists require a new model which demonstrates the existence of equilibrium even under an ideal form of capitalism; otherwise the concept of marginal utility implies that under certain assumed conditions capital and labour are remunerated in proportion to their respective contributions to production. The Fabians sought a solution by extending Ricardo's theory of rent, which concluded that agricultural tenants were exploited by landlords, to the relationship between workers and capitalists in industry. Thus the Fabians developed a theory of exploitation not dependent on the labour theory of value.[3] It was first put forward by Sydney Webb in *The Quarterly Journal of Economics* in January 1888 and popularised by Bernard Shaw in the 1889 *Fabian Essays in Socialism*. It became the cornerstone of the Fabian critique of capitalism and eventually constituted the theoretical core of British labourism. Webb (1920), Wallas (1940) and Shaw (1944) in their several introductions to new editions of the *Fabian Essays*, continued to argue that it was a substantial contribution to socialist thought.[4]

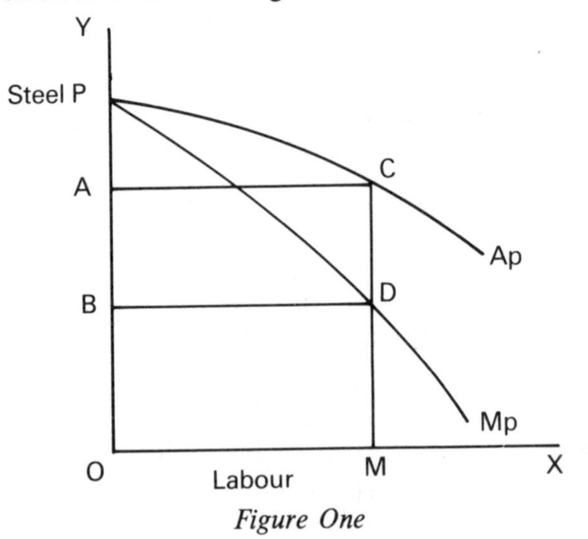

Figure One

Figure One demonstrates the application of Ricardo's theory of rent[5] to capitalist industry. OY measures the quantity of steel (taken as a surrogate for aggregate output), while OX indicates the amount of labour employed. At a given state of technology and with given productive resources, P-Ap represents average product per unit of labour and P-Mp its marginal product. The decline in average product due to the operation of diminishing returns leads to a gap between these schedules. When the quantity of labour is given, output is uniquely determined; for workforce OM, total production is shown by the rectangle ACOM. The difference between the average and the marginal productivity of labour constitutes surplus value, the size of which depends on the elasticity of P-Ap determined by the speed at which diminishing returns occur.

This surplus value can be divided amongst:

(i) economic rent, *e.g.* the extra product created by advantages of the site,

(ii) rent of ability, *e.g.* the extra product created by superior skill relative to unskilled workers. Administration of capital, organisation of industry, supervision and direction of the labour process are all crucial in this context,

(iii) economic interest, *e.g.* the extra product created by use of more or superior quality capital (distinct therefore from the rate of interest), and

(iv) rent of opportunity or profits, *e.g.* the extra product created by the existence of adventitious advantages—for instance, temporary monopolies due to possession of the means of production in a certain form, place or time.

These various rents arise in any society where land, labour or capital vary in quality, but the distinctive feature of capitalism is that owners of the means of production mainly appropriate them. Through skill or organisation certain workers may achieve a quasi-monopoly position, which enables them to secure a portion, but never all, of the rents of ability. Moreover, conventional definitions of skill are positively correlated with education, which is unequally distributed to the advantage of capitalists' families. Therefore returns to factors of production are weighted against those with only labour power to sell.

By extending Ricardian rent theory the Fabians provided a common framework for analysis of all incomes. Exploitation arises not from appropriation of labour's surplus value by capital but from the fact that income from property accrues to a small minority of the population. Identical commodities sold at the same price often incur different costs of production, so that a producer's surplus (termed rent by the Fabians) emerges on the goods and services generated at lower cost. This constitutes an argument for nationalisation of rents which are not necessary to induce production. Consequently the Fabians believed that their theory of rent destroys the assumptions on which private property is justified. The construction of a non-exploitative economy depends upon an equal division of property income, which is possible only when the state owns the means of production. The Fabians advocated state appropriation of the various types of rent, which they believed was already occurring in late nineteenth-century Britain through a series of non-violent, constitutional measures directed by non-socialists unaware of their long-term effects.

Thus the Fabians developed their own concept of capitalist exploitation, which is compatible with any theory of value. It demonstrates that, contrary to the assertion of orthodox economists though in accord with the utility theory they espouse, factors are not rewarded in proportion to the contribution they make to wealth creation since there is an unearned increment accruing to owners of capital. Therefore capitalists enjoy a class monopoly even in perfectly competitive markets (which are ceasing to exist for other reasons).

Admitting that the returns on capital may be analysed through rent theory, that differential returns accrue to firms employing superior capital and that these returns constitute private income for shareholders, it need not follow that they are unearned, for conventional economists could argue that more efficient capital is created by individual abstinence and risk bearing. The Fabians required additional arguments to counter the assertion that capitalists are active agents of production who supply capital through saving. Olivier (1888) provided them; he accepted that capital contributes to production when used in conjunction with labour, that present capital derives from abstinence from current claims and that the accumulation of capital is essential for economic growth, but he denied that the existence of capitalists as a class is thereby justified because:

(i) saving is an activity that can be performed collectively by the community via taxation rather than by wealthy individuals,

(ii) little or no sacrifice is involved in the majority of saving which is undertaken by the rich. Indeed it is a convenience allowing them to consume at a later date what they cannot easily consume immediately,

(iii) capitalist accumulation is unjust; by investing, capitalists obtain an enduring tribute from workers (in the form of lower consumption) for using their savings, which only their use can prevent from perishing, while they retain an undiminished claim to the original saving.

Olivier concluded that capital is necessary for productive efficiency yet capitalists are not, except in so far as they undertake managerial and administrative functions that can be separated from investment and performed by salaried employees.

Individualistic anarchists claim that *laissez faire* works justly once equality is established, but socialists believe that inequality reappears without state intervention since they assume that inequality is natural yet undesirable. Fabians used their theory of rent to prove that exploitation is inevitable even under ideal capitalist conditions, but they supported it with additional observations:

(i) The price mechanism responds only to demands made effective by purchasing power, so that an inequitable outcome is inevitable given pre-existing distributive inequality.

(ii) Prices fail to reflect the relative intensity of the disutilities incurred by productive agents; for instance, a greater sacrifice is involved in performing long hours of monotonous work for a low wage than in the rich's decision to save.

(iii) Capitalism developed historically under a state of inequality, which it is likely to perpetuate if not intensify. The operation of an economy, in which production for profit predominates, necessarily accentuates the class division between a wealthy minority and a propertyless majority. Inequality is constantly reproduced as those who begin with material advantages possess both the incentive and resources to maintain their privileged position. Thus Lewis (1949) wrote:

> 'the price mechanism rewards people according to the scarcity of the resources they own, but it does not itself contain any mechanism for equalising the distribution of scarcities. For justice in distribution we clearly have to summon the forces of the state'.

Such arguments strengthen the fundamental Fabian theory of exploitation based upon a generalisation of Ricardo's theory of rent, which stresses the crucial role of the monopoly ownership of land and capital, and the need to remove it by progressive taxation and a gradual extension of state enterprise. The Fabian pioneers continued to believe that their contribution was superior to that of Marx, but latter-day Marxists see it as a static attempt to bypass the analysis of capitalism as a dynamic system propelled by its own contradictions. Unlike Marx, the Fabians failed to integrate their concept of exploitation with a theory of aggregate demand explaining economic crises. It can hardly be an accident that they developed no theory of economic growth nor that they failed to suggest a remedy when confronted with the major depression of the interwar years.

THE FABIANS AND ECONOMIC CRISES

The 1909 Minority Report of the Royal Commission on the Poor Law, of which Beatrice Webb was a member, recommended on Fabian initiative an increase in government expenditure when the trade cycle entered its downward phase, a precursor of Keynesian proposals. However, the Fabians failed to develop the theoretical implications of their proposal nor did they construct a model of cyclical fluctuations. They regarded economic crises as examples of the injustice caused by capitalism but not as threats to the existence of the entire economic system. Sydney Webb argued that unemployment was the most vivid manifestation of working-class poverty, permanently remediable only by collective ownership of industry which releases profits to finance personal spending; purchasing power is raised and the danger of slumps arising from underconsumption is averted. As a short term palliative, he advocated government construction programmes planned over a ten year period and accelerated when the national unemployment rate climbed above four per cent. Such schemes could be financed by borrowing from idle balances ('unemployed capital') in a depression or taxing the rich during a boom. The British Labour Party did not respond to these ideas, which were regarded as 'tinkering with capitalism', while public job creation suffered from its association with nineteenth-century relief work. Moreover, after 1918 there was no cycle just continuous unemployment, and the finance of public works in a permanent depression raised difficulties. The Fabians possessed no monetary theory, so that increased taxation seemed to add to industry's burdens and borrowing to divert resources that were already productively employed. The chief Fabian contribution to macroeconomics was the notion of under-consumption arising from inequality. If wages are kept down, a lack of purchasing power leads to overproduction, but if wages rise, a crisis of profitability occurs.[6]

THE TRANSITION TO SOCIALISM

Any group predicting a transition to socialism must list the forces operating in and against that direction. Some theory is then required to establish which tendency is likely to prevail. The Fabians discounted the possibility that capitalist crises will increasingly threaten the system's existence, emphasising instead the contradiction between the potential power of the working class and its social condition. They visualised workers using their votes to control the terms of exchange for labour and working conditions, thus gradually acquiring industrial, through political, democracy. Fabians felt that class conflict could be lessened, and possibly removed, by parliamentary methods based upon universal suffrage.[7] They were optimistic about the prospects for peaceful change and did not take seriously dangers of counter-revolution in Britain. They anticipated that after a learning period working-class enfranchisement would enforce the adoption of socialist measures.

The nineteenth-century conventional wisdom of the minimal state remained plausible so long as the state was undemocratic or *laissez faire* principles were desirable. The existence of a central authority armed with coercive power reinforces exploitation if it is undemocratic or if workers elect capitalists to represent them. The Fabians accepted that the existence of capitalism and inequality corrupts the democratic decision-making process, but argued that universal suffrage creates the possibility of electing workers and socialists to positions of power. They recognised the crucial task of persuading people to use their potential strength effectively but believed that state coercion was now potentially anti-capitalist. The collective will can express broad principles on matters affecting the whole nation, although the Webbs saw legislation as a distinct craft; the problem for socialists is to secure experts' services yet subject them to popular control. Despite the subversion of parliamentary institutions by capitalism, Fabians believed that such institutions could change economic systems and social structures. They saw history as a river flowing slowly yet inexorably towards socialism (the inevitability of gradualness), with Fabians demonstrating its direction and removing obstacles to its flow. Their failure to develop a theory of capitalist crises led to the implicit yet vital conclusion that socialism is built on the success rather than the failure of capitalism.

The Fabians discerned an alteration in the state's character in response to its changed role. It evolves away from its function as the body with monopoly use of legitimate force into a set of institutions dealing with the administration of public services. Its emergence as employer, producer, and provider of welfare transforms its traditional violent nature; the capitalist state rests on coercion, the socialist state on service.

Therefore the Fabian vision of the transition to socialism was of a gradual transformation made possible by universal suffrage and the extension of government control over industry. The advantages of collective enterprise are numerous; the ethics of professional management could prevent corporate selfishness and enable the coordination of administration, the government could restrict consumption by raising prices or stimulate it through subsidies, greater equality results from the abolition of private profits, while contact with the socialist state cultivates the sense of community essential to socialism. Thus Fabians saw nationalisation as a necessary but not a sufficient condition for transition.

The Fabian theory of the state contrasts sharply with that of Marx. Marxists see capitalist governments as instruments used by the property-owning class to maintain its hegemony; since class attitudes are determined by self-interest, capitalists never accept socialism by reason. Consequently they have to be dispossessed, often by force, while the proletariat's false consciousness must be removed to prepare for the revolutionary struggle. British socialists found this argument difficult to accept and after the achievement of universal suffrage concentrated upon parliamentary activity. The Fabians sought converts by providing evidence of capitalism's malfunctioning together with suggested socialist remedies, so that their ultimate goal was a revolution of reason.

Sydney Webb stipulated four conditions to be satisfied before the implementation of major change:

(i) democratic — it is supported by a majority,
(ii) gradual — it involves minimum dislocation,
(iii) ethical — it is not regarded by the majority as immoral,
(iv) constitutional and peaceful (in Britain, at least).

No single legislative reform by itself threatens the existence of capitalism, but their cumulative effect is to produce socialism. Transition occurs gradually with no final reform nor a clear frontier between the alternative modes of production, but Fabians saw it as an inevitable process independent of individual desires. They believed that in a parliamentary democracy based on universal suffrage the state is a neutral agency that can be used by a majority to achieve social transformation. Because the working class in Britain constitutes a majority, its piecemeal reforms can strip away the privileges of capitalists and create socialism by peaceful evolution.

In contrast, Marxists argue that once reforms seriously threaten capitalists' prerogatives, they resort to intimidation, repression and ultimately abolition of workers' democratic rights rather than witness the erosion of their position. When this happens labour requires a revolutionary organisation to prevent the loss of its previous advances. Moreover, the gradual conversion of minds is at best a long process, while social improvements may improve the grievances which provide socialists with their support. The Fabian theory of transition appears problematic in the face of historical experience, the weight of which suggests that evolutionary socialists tend to be pushed by the pressures of achieving electoral majorities to abandon their most fundamental tenet — socialisation of the means of production.

THE FABIAN VISION OF A SOCIALIST ECONOMY

The Fabians were paternalistic, seeing the nation as a family headed in future by a benign state providing the basic necessities for all. Governments assume the character of cooperative societies, becoming less coercive the more they engage in national housekeeping, so that the tenor of politics changes as social administration is geared to general rather than class needs. Fabians saw a role for private enterprise under socialism as the pioneer of innovation; a fringe of small, profit-seeking ventures exist alongside nationalised industries, which are allowed to survive until they become sufficiently established for transfer into public ownership. As nationalisation occurs on a sector-by-sector basis, the payment of compensation is expedient even though the incomes of capitalists and landlords are unearned.

The state becomes an almost universal employer, taking over private corporations whose shareholders can be bought out with no more dislocation than is involved in the purchase of shares on the Stock Exchange. Capitalists unconsciously pave the way for their abolition by creating joint stock companies susceptible to nationalisation. Fabian dislike of *laissez faire* led to a wholesale rejection of liberalism, which they replaced with reorganisation of society by the state, enabling coordination of administration and conscious planning. Such a doctrine appealed to many bureaucrats, technicians and industrial managers.

Fabians emphasised the efficiency gains derived from economies of scale and consistently opposed workers' control of industry since this 'seeks to establish socialism by private enterprise'. The Webbs argued that workers possessed neither the desire nor the capability to run businesses. They defined socialist industrial democracy as the control of publicly-owned industry by professional managers accountable to the community through supervision by an elected parliament, local authorities and consumer cooperatives. The structure of nationalised corporations is determined by the scope of their activities and the proportion of the population affected by them. The Fabians recognised the dangers of unresponsive bureaucracy latent within their proposals; thus the Webbs in their *Constitution for the Socialist Commonwealth of Great Britain* proposed the creation of two separate parliaments, one to preside over political, and the other over economic and social, affairs underpinned by a structure of local government units capable of controlling efficiently the producers of goods and services. The precise size and location of these units depends upon the character of the commodities provided.

Fabians rejected the concept of irremediable class conflict, since it denies the identity of consumer interests that capitalism obscures and on which socialism will rest. They failed to meet the charge that 'repressed people would carry their repression into a reconstructed society', while they reduced the role of workers to spectators in the process of social transformation, the key roles being performed by a professional elite who set guidelines and train future administrators. However, they stressed the importance of securing popular approval for socialist reforms. A legal guarantee of work for all (by removing the perpetual insecurity associated with a market economy) responds to human needs and helps to attract public support. These considerations lead to analysis of the political influence wielded by the Fabians in their attempt to achieve socialist transition.

THE FABIANS' POLITICAL STRATEGY

Beatrice Webb was influential in reorientating Fabian thinking away from theoretical economics towards the history and development of institutions. She felt that 'frictions' were more important than 'laws' over much of the subject matter of economics, while many of the assumptions about human behaviour and interaction that underlie economic analysis are contradicted by empirical observation. The Fabians came to see the development of local government, trade unions and co-operative societies as 'a spontaneous undergrowth of social tissue' advancing towards socialism, so that they concentrated upon advocacy of a programme of piecemeal reforms.

Fabians sought to avoid an awakening of class consciousness, which might impede the spread of their principles through the political and administrative organs of capitalist society. However, they helped to launch the I.L.P., cooperated with the Labour Representation Committee, assisted trade union activity, shaped the course of the Progressive Party on London County Council and tirelessly preached socialism. They never issued resounding declarations of conflict but never undertook to protect capitalism. They did not believe that an imminent capitalist crisis due to its own logic of operation was likely, but thought that socialisation would be a slow process altering gradually the attitudes of all classes. Consequently they focussed on problems within the scope of immediate politics, publishing numerous research tracts exposing poverty and injustice. They sought to persuade whoever would listen; they lectured, lobbyed and pamphleteered, and established contact with influential individuals. They stressed their willingness to co-operate to achieve practical reforms more than their ultimate hostility to the established order. Essentially they become unofficial public servants, since action through the bureaucracy, whose growth in numbers and influence they foresaw and approved, fitted their scheme of state socialism.

Despite Shaw's assistance in forming the I.L.P. in 1893,[8] the Fabian attitude to the emergent Labour Representation Committee was one of benevolent passivity before 1914. However, those Fabians supporting participation in the First World War grew close to the official Labour leadership, primarily due to the work of Sydney Webb on the War Emergency: Workers National Committee.[9] Through this body he became the guiding force in formulating a consistent socialist programme and in reorganising the Labour Party during 1917 and 1918. The war provided a new impetus to Fabian tactics of permeation, the W.E.C. being formed to implement a strategy of investigation and deputation on behalf of the working class to politicians, civil servants and the media. Webb's knowledge of social administration and the minutiae of labour problems, together with his organisational ability and lack of personal ambition, made him the W.E.C.'s unofficial leader. He used it to project his ideas and to consolidate a collection of interest groups into a unified labour movement under socialist leadership, drawing up the Labour Party constitution accepted in 1918 with its accompanying manifesto, *Labour and the New Social Order*. These wrote evolutionary socialism into both the Labour Party's objectives and its immediate programme.

The constitution and the programme rested on an ideology indicting capitalism (the famous Clause Four) and promised the initial mitigation, and ultimate removal, of the inequality and deprivation it created. *Labour and the New Social Order* postulated four foundations of a future socialist economy, each with deep roots in Fabian thinking: universal enforcement of a national minimum income, democratic organisation of industry (not workers' control but progressive elimination of private capitalists' authority by state planning), a revolution in national finance and expropriation of surplus wealth.[10] Although the

Fabians remained a small elite never seeking a mass membership, by 1918 the Labour Party had adopted a programme that reflected their overall philosophy and specific economic theories. In order to generate popular support for such a programme the Fabians devoted considerable attention to education; for instance, the Webbs founded the London School of Economics in 1894 with funds over which they exercised exclusive control.

CONCLUSION

Marxism proved difficult to popularise in late nineteenth-century Britain, the most prosperous country in the world, which had enjoyed the rapid economic growth of the Railway Age and the advent of universal suffrage since its turbulent transition to factory production. The Fabians developed a form of socialism acceptable in a relatively rich country, making it easy for members of the middle class to become socialists while retaining their privileged life style.[11] However, their claim to have 'broken the spell of Marxism in Britain' is exaggerated because few Britons had understood it, so the Fabians had the arena largely to themselves. Hyndman could not, while Engels would not, refute Wicksteed's critique of the labour theory of value yet the Fabians accepted it. Consequently economists were left with the notion that Marx was 'all wrong abour surplus value' and therefore unworthy of study. Thus no sizeable proportion of the British Left adopted even a modified version of Marxism until the 1930s.

The Fabians aided a change in social objectives involving abandonment of *laissez faire* and acceptance of a partially planned economy with greater equality as one of its objectives. They enabled Britain to assimilate these aims without a great shock. They stood opposed to the central values of nineteenth-century British political culture, a set of conventions fortified by its apparent success in raising Britain to the pinnacle of nations. The two crucial conventions were:

(i) *economic internationalism*, comprising an economic theory of comparative costs which on certain assumptions supported free trade and the international mobility of resources, a penumbra of ethical values embodied pre-eminently by Cobden, and an ideology of powerful interest groups whose profits depended upon internationalism. Due to its early monopoly of industrial production, Britain locked itself into the world economy; the City of London operated as the global centre of finance, while the Bank of England managed the international gold standard.

(ii) *minimal government*, resting on the partial analysis of efficient resource allocation through pricing, the political principle of individual liberty and the self-interest of elites who felt their position to be challenged, at least potentially, by state intervention. This overall paradigm appeared to be rarified by a belief that *laissez faire* was the cause of Britain's economic triumphs. The doctrine of minimal government possessed such a strong hold that the Labour Party's commitment to state socialism was never implemented in practice until after the impact of the Second World War.

These two beliefs — in economic internationalism and minimal government — constituted British economic orthodoxy, which was partly a creation of economists but more a product of the views held by powerful institutions and interest groups concerning their own and the economy's operation. These form a body of opinion that no government challenges lightly. The Fabians, however, provided such a challenge and the weakening of faith in the twin pillars of nineteenth-century orthodoxy is a phenomenon for which they can be held partly responsible. Thus they assisted a gradual transformation in Britain's political objectives.

The Fabians definition of socialism triumphed within the Labour Party and was generally accepted as the focus for attack by non-socialists. Given the weakness of Marxism in Britain, it was crucial for Fabian success that they possessed theories of exploitation and transition, while their rivals had no alternative philosophy out of which a tactical approach to immediate issues emerged. This advantage proved decisive after 1914 when the Labour movement had to give detailed answers to the specific questions posed by the war and its aftermath. The influence of the Fabians, particularly the Webbs, was great between 1914 and 1918, but they proved less effective in the inter-war period when the relevance of their theories was more problematic.

APPENDIX: EUROPEAN REVISIONISM

A corpus of radical economic theories termed 'Revisionism' developed in the late nineteenth century on the European continent. This was similar to British Fabianism despite the significant difference that it originated in direct attempts to revise Marx's ideas. In particular the Revisionists sought to replace revolution by gradual reform as the route to socialism, but unlike the Fabians they had to argue within an environment dominated by Marxism. The most famous Revisionist was Bernstein (1899).

Bernstein believed that many of Marx's prophecies remained unfulfilled; for instance, small business had not disappeared, acute class conflict had not developed, while workers' material conditions were improving. From these observations he argued that an appeal to revolutionary force was ineffective in a situation where higher living standards and increased democratisation of government made violent change both unlikely and undesirable. The need was to develop working-class industrial and political organisations to achieve immediate ameliorating reforms, in the knowledge that no capitalist crisis was imminent.

Bernstein repudiated some of Marx's fundamental postulates. He denied the overriding importance of the economic interpretation of history by giving an independent causal role to ethical factors. He believed that humanity possesses increasing control over social forces as development proceeds, so that economic forces become less, and ideology more, important over time. Moreover, he did not accept Marx's theory of social class; he thought that the population was becoming increasingly differentiated rather than being polarised into two groups. Class conflict can hardly be the moving force of history if class distinctions are frequently non-existent and rapidly breaking down.

Bernstein was equally critical of the syndicalist ideas prevalent in certain countries. He argued that workers' control was impossible as it would destroy managerial authority and undesirable since trade unions were 'unsocialistic corporate bodies' with interests narrower than those of the community as a whole. He believed that parliamentary democracy would propel the transition to socialism; by giving all voters a partnership in the nation, the state ceases to be a class instrument and patriotism becomes a rational attitude for workers. Therefore democracy is not merely a condition but the essence of socialism, which will be attained through skilful use of the ballot box. Marxists argue that capitalist governments are primarily agents of class rule and that capitalists use their wealth to ensure the continuance of private property relations. Bernstein replied that such an argument was previously true but had been invalidated by universal suffrage, which could make all voters equally powerful in selecting the government, and had destroyed class rule by enabling universal participation in the political process. He rejected the Marxist view that capitalist governments display inevitable class bias, and believed that both capitalists and workers can be induced by moral appeals to promote the general interests of society.

The Revisionists did not merely substitute 'peaceful evolution' for 'revolution', but directly attacked many of the intellectual foundations of Marxism. By arguing that economic development promotes not crises but stability, they implied that capitalism had never been more flourishing so that the 'inevitability' of socialism was reduced to a tame 'desirability'. The Revisionists' arguments provoked a debate within the German Social Democratic Party, which eventually ended in compromise; its leader, Bebel, denounced Revisionism, but framed resolutions on contentious issues in a form acceptable to Revisionists. Bernstein even entered the Reichstag with Social Democratic support. His arguments are essentially a less developed, but more explicitly anti-Marxist, version of Fabian political economy.

NOTES

1 *Das Kapital* was not published in English until 1887.
2 Wicksteed (1894) was one of the earliest proponents of the marginal productivity theory of distribution.
3 Indeed it can be held whether a labour, cost of production or marginal utility theory of value is adopted.
4 In 1920 Webb wrote: 'the part of the book that comes most triumphantly through the ordeal is the economic analysis. Tested by a whole generation

of further experience and criticism, I conclude that in 1889 we knew our political economy and that our political economy was sound'.

5 Chapter Four discusses this theory in greater detail.

6 Hobson (1900), never a Fabian, was an exception among British socialists in linking capitalist crises to exploitation and war through his theory of under-consumption. He argued that slumps are caused by a deficiency of working-class purchasing power, which leads to capital export, international rivalry and ultimately war; if incomes were more evently distributed, slumps and the foreign investment to which they give rise would disappear.

7 Fabians, like Marxists, define classes in terms of ownership of the means of production.

8 Bernard Shaw, representing the Fabian Society, proposed the motion to establish the existence of the Independent Labour Party at an 1893 conference.

9 Henceforth abbreviated to 'W.E.C.'

10 'Surplus wealth' in this context is analagous to the Fabian concept of 'rent'.

11 Shaw (1937) wrote: 'should you become a socialist, you will not be committed to any change in your private life; nor indeed will you find yourself able to make changes that would be of the smallest use in that direction'.

7 Syndicalism and Guild Socialism

Trade unions developed late in France in relation to other European countries, and because they operated in an economy with a small industrial sector they achieved only a low degree of unionisation. Nineteenth-century France was typically a nation of artisans, clerks and peasants because large-scale capitalist industry remained confined to a few centres. Consequently a broad base of economic conservatism prevented the emergence of large disciplined political parties, and parliamentary strategies revolved around the formation of temporary coalitions between small interest groups. As a result French socialists became closer to, and attained, political office sooner than in other countries but at the cost of accepting capitalist constraints because of their minority position. In these circumstances an alternative political economy, Syndicalism, developed in response to workers' disillusion with Fabian democracy and their lack of faith in the possibility of capitalist breakdown as postulated by Marx. Despite the absence of a large, unified labour movement, workers sought to transform economic relationships by industrial activity.

THE POLITICAL BACKGROUND CONDUCIVE TO SYNDICALISM

In the United States a different social pattern proved equally unconducive to the development of mass socialism. The large agrarian sector formed an anti-socialist force, rapid growth of industry coupled to the existence of the frontier reduced class friction and substantial immigration weakened trade union hegemony. The realisation of American economic potentialities impressed business attitudes on the national culture, so that most workers felt themselves to be exploiters of their individual opportunities and shared their employers' outlook. Their collective organisations took the form of business unions cooperating with capitalists except during collective bargaining, which focussed largely upon questions of wages and hours.

However, an alternative Syndicalism emerged in 1893 as a breakaway from the Knights of Labour.[1] Termed the Industrial Workers of the World and headed by De Leon, it sought destruction of the capitalist state through class conflict culminating in revolution. Its numerical strength lay in the Western Federation of Miners, whose radicalism was a reaction to a harsh environment, and it gained a series of strike successes through a spirit of uncompromising warfare. It was Syndicalist in espousing direct action and seeing its role as the harbinger of a socialist society, yet it collapsed after the First World War owing to defections among its membership to communism, to internal dissension and to the application in several states of criminal laws designed to prohibit its activities.

Syndicalism also spread to Austria, Belgium, Ireland, Italy and Spain, but was most significant in France where it became the official ideology of the largest trade union federation (the C.G.T.) In 1896 and 1902 the C.G.T advocated use of the general strike, while in the 1906 Charter of Amiens it affirmed its independence from the French Socialist Party and adopted the following Syndicalist strategy:

(i) strikes by individual trade unions comparable to manoeuvres,[2]

(ii) a cessation of work on a given day by all workers comparable to general manoeuvres,[2]

(iii) a general and complete stoppage of work placing the proletariat in revolution against capitalism. Given the minority status of French labour, a seizure of power could only be achieved by a disciplined group of collectively organised workers. Trade unions, as the embodiment of collective organisation, are not only agents of combat but also the creators of a socialist economy.

Syndicalism was a protest against authority, compromise, established political and industrial procedures, and the apparent ineffectiveness of democracy. Its philosophy centred on revolution as the outcome of a class war waged by trade unions, which are destined to supplant the state machinery. These sentiments were the product of a spontaneous workers' movement, the heir to France's revolutionary tradition. Subsequently intellectuals, of whom Georges Sorel was the most famous, supplied a supporting framework of economic theory.

SOREL AND SYNDICALIST THEORY

Sorel claimed to be the workers' student rather than their teacher, but he became the prominent Syndicalist theorist. He saw his role as stripping Marxism to its essential core, class struggle. Reforms of capitalism should be avoided, as they may blur the lines of class demarcation, while parliamentary action is slow, based on compromise and enmeshes the working class in its enemies' procedures. Democracy seeks to create the delusion of national unity above the class struggle even if only on the basis of agreements to differ. Political parties represent a constructed intellectual consensus across classes in contrast to classes themselves, which are based on homogeneity in the conditions of life. In Sorel's neo-Marxist model such bonds are the only ones that survive changing circumstances, so that the possibility of social transformation depends upon the outcome of class conflict rather than upon political activity, which accepts existing state institutions. Sorel saw the purpose of Syndicalism as revolt against capitalism not the amelioration of workers' conditions under it. If socialists accept government procedures they inevitably become their defenders, supporting the status quo against disorder and so betray the working class.

An alternative strategy seeks to develop distinct proletarian institutions as effective weapons in the contemporary class struggle, yet these are simultaneously designed to exercise increasing authority over industrial administration. Ultimately capitalism becomes subordinate and its crucial operations are transferred to working-class bodies. Trade unions can only undertake such a task if they become educational agencies, regenerating their members' culture of solidarity and socialism in preparation for their future role. Thus Sorel thought unions to be indispensable in the existing warfare between capital and labour, but more importantly in the long run to be capable of abolishing wage labour. To this end, they must struggle for total working-class emancipation, support every movement within the proletariat and recruit all labour into their ranks.

The Syndicalist theory of transition rests on the use of a general strike to produce chaos. Sorel advocated strike activity as the central socialist strategy, extending from local to industrial and ultimately to national level. The general strike serves three purposes:

(i) It gives significance to individual disputes which are seen as skirmishes within a larger campaign.

(ii) It provides concrete expression of the fact that socialism is not built upon gradual changes but requires a complete transformation in social relations.

(iii) It underlines the redundancy of political reforms.

Therefore, to Syndicalists, all strikes are educational, disciplinary and symbolic, reinforcing heroism, sacrifice and unity. Sorel argued that a general strike possesses two dimensions; it is a myth giving revolutionaries confidence but is also the means of achieving social change. He believed that armed violence would be an essential feature of a successful revolution, since it provides momentum for the general strike. He advocated sabotage as an additional working-class weapon which inflicts confusion, as well as financial and physical damage, upon capitalists. Trade unions must engage in anti-patriotic and anti-militaristic campaigns, since class, and not nation, constitutes the crucial divide; police and soldiers, although essentially proletarian, form a potential strike-breaking force. After a revolutionary struggle culminating in a successful general strike which reduces profits to zero, existing economic and political institutions would be replaced by a federal structure based on local organisation of producers. Workers' control of industry would be operated by the relevant trade union, which sends delegates to coordinating committees brought together in a general labour federation. Syndicalism was adopted by the C.G.T. as its ideology until 1914; elsewhere it was less broadly based but was not negligible.

Syndicalism was a philosophy based on action rather than an economic theory. It stressed the virtues of attack, audacity, imagination and the role of a conscious minority in imposing its views. It was anti-democratic in devaluing the functions of conventional political procedures and anti-intellectual in mistrusting the adoption of programmes backed by a corpus of theory. It appealed to workers' instincts by promising them power within their immediate environment and believed that capitalism, already decaying, can and should be overthrown by violence.

Such a strategy encounters formidable problems. It is by no

means certain that strikes raise workers' consciousness; some do but others, particularly those ending in defeat, may deplete trade union membership and convert revolutionaries into reformists. The aftermath of the British general strike in 1926 provides an illustration of the demoralising effects of defeat. Syndicalism is open to the further objection that in a general strike workers lose their livelihood while eliminating profits and they are more likely to face starvation since capitalists usually enjoy the possession of greater resources. Therefore labour is under greater compulsion to concede quickly and occupies a consequently weaker bargaining position. Industrial dispute statistics support this contention, as the longer the duration of the strike, the greater the proportion that employers win. The obstacles to a successful general strike strategy are great and they multiply when the possibility of counteraction by the state and by capitalists is considered. Syndicalists were largely prepared to let future economic organisation look after itself. They possessed a distinctive transitional policy — progressive encroachment of workers' control through strike activity to oust capital and transform the state — but their alternative was left in the vague terms of an anarchism of producer groups, whereby individual workers would find affiliation, responsibility and satisfaction.

SYNDICALISM IN BRITAIN

Syndicalism spread from France to Britain, where it obtained formal organisation in the Socialist Labour Party formed in 1903 by James Connolly. Its membership was mainly confined to Scotland although after 1910 Tom Mann disseminated Syndicalist ideas to a wider audience through his journal, *The Industrial Syndicalist*. These ideas found a receptive audience before the First World War when a fall in real wages, combined with the apparent ineffectiveness of Labour Party and trade union leaders, led to a growing number of industrial disputes conducted with increased violence on both sides. British Syndicalists advocated 'direct action' through which unions used the strike weapon to capture political power and thereafter control industry. They saw class collaboration as a method of maintaining labour's subordination. They set two short-term objectives:

(i) to achieve a militant trade union policy. They partially succeeded as a series of extensive industrial disputes occurred between 1908 and 1914 largely in response to the failure of money wages to keep pace with prices, so that real wages fell at a time when the wealthy were becoming ostentatiously richer;

(ii) to restructure the craft unions into a few large organisations, each covering one industry and standing ready to take it over. Some progress occurred; the Miners Federation was formed in 1908, the Transport Workers Federation in 1910 and the Railwaymens Union in 1913, while the three subsequently created the Triple Alliance. The T.U.C. declared in favour of amalgamations in 1911 and 1912, while in 1914 an unofficial movement developed within building to form one industrial union. More generally, the labour movement learnt in the years before 1914 that the more extensive and potentially disruptive a strike, the more likely was its success, in that government intervention leading to a compromise became more probable.

In these ways Syndicalists exerted an influence on British trade unionism but their numbers remained small and they did not survive in any strength after the defeat of the general strike in 1926. Guild Socialism was more significant in Britain. Its leading exponents were middle-class intellectuals[3] dissatisfied with the legislation of the 1906 Parliament and the performance of the Labour Party. They sought to combine Syndicalism with the Ruskin-Morris belief that work should be a creative, life-enhancing experience, fearing that both Fabians and Marxists gave too much power to the state. They thus constructed a distinctive political economy which retains contemporary significance.

THE POLITICAL ECONOMY OF THE GUILD SOCIALISTS

Guild Socialists stressed the centrality of production. They pointed out that people spend more time producing than consuming, so that the organisation of industry is more important than distribution. Yet under capitalism, labour power is a commodity and after its sale workers effectively renounce control over workplace conditions and the disposal of commodities. The Guild Socialists argued that parliamentary democracy is an empty formality without the backing of industrial democracy, but felt that the latter requires abolition of the wage system. When capitalism is superseded, trade unions can enter into partnership with the state to create effective industrial self-government. Therefore Guild Socialism creates a framework for the co-management of production by government and unions. Ownership of the means of production ultimately rests with the community but the unions possess day-to-day authority over economic processes.[4] For workshop democracy to be achieved, the labour force must elect and control its managers, so that unions become statutory guilds exerting authority over the methods of production. They effectively exercise the functions of self-governing corporations; because they embrace all workers from elected managers to labourers, they constitute associations of independent producers. Democracy becomes a reality embodying its fundamental principles in workplace relations.

Participation means playing an active role in making the decisions that affect one's life, and Guild Socialists argued that four features of capitalism ensure that it cannot enable such participation:

(i) workers surrender control over the organisation of production,

(ii) workers are subject within the labour process to a disciplinary procedure that they cannot influence directly,

(iii) workers possess no claim to the commodities they produce,

(iv) wages are paid only when employment is profitable for capitalists, so that workers suffer insecurity, their livelihood being determined by such phenomena as changes in demand and technical progress over which they exert little impact.

The Guild Socialists accepted Marx's theory of class conflict, but departed from orthodox Marxism in their vision of the transition to socialism. They saw trade unions as an embryonic form of post-capitalist organisation, in which economic equality defined as maximum participation is a prerequisite for political equality. Therefore they sought to provide workers with:

(i) a claim upon the product of their work,

(ii) control over productive processes,

(iii) payment as human beings, whether employed or not.

In these circumstances labour ceases to be an object manipulated in the service of profit. By posing a comprehensive alternative to the existing organisation of industry, the Guild Socialists revealed the poverty of those deprived of the chance to realise their creative potentialities. Only through providing workers with control over their products and job environments, can the exercise of critical faculties be restored. Effective control can only be based on power, *i.e.* the possession of authority and information.

Guild Socialists sought to remove the power external to workers' employment; otherwise servility remains. Abolition of capitalists and the transfer to workers of control over the production and sales processes enables 'wages' (*i.e.* what capitalists are constrained to give) to be replaced by 'pay' (*i.e.* the entitlement of those rendering a service). Producers can rely on an income irrespective of factors — such as health and trade conditions — which they cannot influence, and industrial motivation becomes based upon service rather than financial self-interest. Trade unions provide the basis for such a transformation, ultimately becoming guilds exercising industrial authority and incorporating all those involved in production including managerial and professional staff.

Guild Socialists shared with Marx the belief that ownership of the means of production determines the political superstructure, so that transition to socialism hinges on a transformation of the labour process. Political power derives from economic power, defined as the ability to exploit or to resist exploitation, so that liberation from capitalism is possible only through industrial pressure exerted by trade unions. Class struggle is a necessary but transient phase in socialist transformation;thus Cole (1913) advocated social change through industrial activity rather than political reforms, given the existence of a class society. Guild Socialists, like Syndicalists, relied upon industrial unionism to create a structure for workers' control, which operates upwards from the shopfloor where foremen and managers are elected for finite periods. Nationalisation is a necessary, but not a sufficient, condition which the industrial trade union can harness to remove its members' position of economic servitude.

The Guild Socialists shared the Syndicalist view that strikes are an effective weapon in the class struggle and that social peace is a fraudulent concept under capitalism, where only a temporary truce between capital and labour is possible. Because economic power shapes political power, state sovereignty is a myth and parliamentary action ineffective. The state is only one association among many. Guild Socialists saw the economy as a complex of organised institutions, each formed to satisfy individual needs. Representation could only be functional, never universal, so that the notion of a comprehensive state with absolute competence is absurd. Governments are associations incorporating all citizens concerned with what they share in common, *i.e.* their role as consumers. Collective groups provide a bridge between the individual and the state, have their own characteristics, and are logically and historically prior to the state and not created by it.

Therefore the Guild Socialists constructed a political economy incorporating elements of Marxism, Fabianism and Syndicalism. They thought the first too authoritarian and the second too narrow, while the third denied the relevance of the state, seeing production as the only significant economic activity. Aspects of each were needed to achieve a complete theory of socialism, defined as the development of industrial self-government by organised labour. Increasing workers' control of production as an outcome of class conflict ultimately renders capitalists functionless.

The Guild Socialist blueprint consisted of self-governing guilds organised democratically on a workshop basis. Voting becomes more effective since it concerns issues of everyday importance about which workers possess detailed knowledge. The separate guilds are coordinated in an Industrial Guilds Conference, which establishes the basic principles of guild practice. Workers cease to be wage slaves but become creative participants in a functional democracy. The truncated parliament still in existence represents consumers and integrates its activities with those of the producers' guilds through a joint body. The function of the state is to represent consumers, so that producers and consumers (exercising influence through parliament) exert joint control over the ends of production, while workers' guilds determine the means. Cole (1919) formulated a detailed Guild Socialist constitution, under which relations among guilds and between guilds and the state are institutionalised. It is a practical expression of the doctrine of multiple sovereignty; the national executive of each industrial guild sends delegates to a National Guild Congress, which elects half the members to a joint board whose other half represents consumers through members of parliament.

A number of problems, theoretical and practical, arise from the political economy of guild socialism. The Guild Socialists were middle-class intellectuals, perhaps over-optimistic about the possibility of developing creativity in a mass of routine jobs. Their primary objective was maximum human happiness attained by working collectively for a common end and they stressed the centrality of production, in contrast to the exclusive concentration of orthodox economists upon consumption.[5]

Certain detailed questions about the guilds' operation admit no simple answers; for example, would they exploit the public by raising prices in imperfectly competitive markets to maximise their collective income? If so, how might their operations be constrained? How would labour transfer between sectors or be made redundant? What form should taxation take? And, should guilds operate on a national or a local basis? Moreover, the Guild Socialists lacked a theory of transition, so that some advocated reformist, and others revolutionary, tactics. These practical problems surfaced in the only attempt to translate Guild Socialist ideas into reality in Britain: the building guild experiment after the First World War, which perished in the depression.[6]

Many deny the relevance of an analogy between parliamentary and industrial democracy, arguing that business can operate efficiently only with the exercise of managerial expertise and an authoritarian hierarchy of workplace relations to enforce discipline. Industrial decision-making may be a public matter susceptible to sectional abuse if confined to a specific labour force; thus lawyers duplicate their work at a considerable resource opportunity cost under a system of professional self-governance. Guild Socialism advocated that workers become the source of industrial authority, yet some economists dispute that employment in an enterprise confers the knowledge essential for decision-making. Any conception of workplace democracy based upon imposing a formal structure of parliamentarianism (election of directors and managers, the taking of production and other decisions by ballot etc.) on the existing organisation of production is delusory. Without the return of technical expertise to workers and a reshaping of the division of labour, which imply in combination a new collective mode of production, elections cannot modify employees' dependence upon 'experts', so that they merely choose between the alternatives presented to them. A prerequisite for effective workers' control is the demystifying of technology and the reorganisation of the labour process; it cannot rest on a purely formal parliamentary analogy.

Doubts are also expressed about the Guild Socialists' definition of the state's function as the representative of consumers. Membership of the state is compulsory, so it is unique among the associations that comprise society; the others impose rules and discipline only on members who voluntarily submit, but the state embodies an ultimate authority over all citizens. Even Guild Socialists accepted the need for a coordinating body to represent consumers and define the conditions under which guilds operate. In most industries workers are outnumbered by consumers yet the latter are too scattered to form a power grouping, so that only the state can protect their interests effectively. However, it seems restrictive to postulate consumption as the sole activity providing common interests between citizens, although even this definition permits a potentially wide role for governments by preserving their ultimate right to intervene in the management of industry by workers. Trade unions represent all producers via the Guild Congress and would normally be the dominant partner in decision-making but their authority can never be absolute. Producers and consumers together, *i.e.* the community as a whole, form the final arbiter. The state can only modify social relations in a minor form so long as the wage system remains intact. However, once the concept of labour as a commodity is rejected and workers have gained control of industry following nationalisation, the state can preside over an alteration of those relations. For Guild Socialists, government activity is essentially a permissive rather than an initiating force; in the words of Cole (1913) 'even if the state includes everybody, it is only one association among others, because it cannot include the whole of everybody'.

Many economists attack the principle of workers' control; thus Bell (1949) advanced three objections, which he believed to be unanswerable, to any such programme:

(i) Sections of the labour force in some, probably most,

industries will insist on being involved in the determination of their own wages and conditions, resulting in the implicit or explicit re-emergence of unions primarily concerned with collective bargaining. Trade unions exercising such functions could hardly represent managerial staff simultaneously.

(ii) Management constitutes a separate, specialised function, whose effective exercise demands a measure of authority and power of decision-making.

(iii) A socialised industry exists for the benefit of the whole community rather than that of any sectional influence even its labour force. Shaw (1937) argued that making enterprises the property of their workers merely replaces existing idle shareholders with employed shareholders, who appropriate profit and contribute as little as possible to the central exchequer. It also perpetuates the inequalities based upon firms' differential earning power, which often bear little relation to the relative efforts of the workers involved.

Whatever one's views on the validity of these objections, there can be little doubt that they have been accepted by a majority of the British labour movement since the 1920s. Clegg (1951) made the additional point that inevitable shortcomings in trade union democracy could become powerful weapons of oppression against which individual workers would possess little protection. Certainly the issues of how to register consumer demands in the absence of a conventional price mechanism, how to eliminate earnings differentials between producer groups and how to protect minorities within guilds require greater consideration than the Guild Socialists provided.

THE RECENT REVIVAL OF INTEREST IN GUILD SOCIALISM, AND THE YUGOSLAVIAN EXPERIENCE

Guild Socialism developed as a system of political economy before 1914, but it faced difficulties during the First World War when it was hard to assert the primacy of achieving social transformation through class struggle. Consequently in 1915 the National Guilds League was formed to propogate Guild Socialist views and to develop structures for industrial self-government by organised workers. It experienced a brief resurgence after 1918 but then sank into insignificance. Guild Socialism has become more relevant today as part of the reaction against large organisations and in response to the desire of many workers for greater control over the deployment of their labour power after its hire. This movement of opinion was reflected in the proposals of the Bullock Report for worker directors, and was given impetus by the establishment of a number of experimental workers' cooperatives with government financial support (*e.g.* the Meriden motor-cycle factory and the 'Scottish Daily News' venture). Demands for the extension of workers' control originate from shopfloor pressure that restrains the exercise of employers' authority, and the method of achieving these demands is usually envisaged as the extension of collective bargaining from a partial regulation of the job environment to cover all items of concern to the workforce. Such an extension would enforce a greater measure of accountability upon industrial decision-making.

In response to the increased interest in proposals for workers' control, a number of economists developed theoretical models of self-management. These conclude that an economy of labour-managed enterprises operating under the same technical conditions and the same requirements of free entry and exit as the conventional entrepreneurial economy would be equally capable of attaining the Pareto-optimal allocation of resources.[7] Advocates of self-management, such as Vanek (1970), claim that this conclusion strengthens their case. However, on the more plausible assumption that some form of imperfect competition prevails, labour-managed enterprises may restrict production to maximise earnings per current worker. Conflict can also arise on the issues of charging for external costs and benefits, the rate of investment and the control of inflation. Shackleton (1976) argued that such conflicts could only be resolved by the existence of a state administration acting as a central coordinating mechanism. Theoretical models of self-management indicate that it does not solve the problems faced by industrial economies in itself, but these have not established that it is inherently less efficient on conventional economic criteria than the capitalist or centrally planned alternatives. Self-management also yields wider benefits by extending the frontier of workers' control over their own lives.

Horvat (1968) provides the most detailed analysis of a socialist economy in which enterprises are controlled by workers who attempt to maximise their profit incomes. He believes that workers' control is inevitable, as a feasible economic structure of superior efficiency. He discerns, even under capitalist relations of production, a trend towards increased labour participation in management in response to union demands, the needs of governments and the policy of enlightened employers. He sees this development as the embryo of a future economy which realises the ultimate Marxist goal of free associations of workers as the source of industrial authority, although he feels it unlikely that full-scale worker control will evolve first from monopoly capitalism. He allows the state a role even in the ultimate stage of labour-management, via a planning board which acts as joint entrepreneur in many industrial decisions and sets the overall framework of economic development. Entrepreneurship becomes diffused throughout society, so that no particular workers' collective can claim the total profits generated by market opportunities. The target income distribution is egalitarian, but initially inequality continues as workers require personal incentives to boost productivity. Eventually, however, the participatory spirit becomes dominant, although a central authority remains essential to provide external defence, domestic order and guidelines for socio-economic progress. Horvat advocates, therefore, direct control of enterprises by the labour force, although market operations within a policy framework laid down by the state determine the consequences of their decisions. Such state planning is necessary to prevent the market from breeding disruption by inculcating selfish values which pit one collective against the rest in a struggle for profit.

Yugoslavia possesses the only economy currently utilising labour-management on a large scale. Its adoption did not occur through the application of a theoretical blueprint, but as a means of fostering economic growth in a country with internal antagonisms and hostility to central control. No industrial enterprises rest upon the private ownership of capital and labour-managed enterprises are independent trading agencies which operate in a largely market environment. They obtain capital through self-financing and borrowing from public agencies, with payment of interest on such loans. Depreciation is set aside from current income to preserve assets and the use of accumulated reserves is at the unit's discretion. Managers are responsible to a works council comprising all members of the labour force, which appoints the director of the enterprise for a four year term and establishes its administrative structure. The works council determines income distribution, the volume of reserves and the method of capital funding.

The Yugoslavian economy has been characterised by the determination of enterprises to maintain output and employment despite national economic vicissitudes. Capital accumulation is encouraged by the high level of depreciation funds available for re-investment, the tax advantages of investing from income, the favourable terms for loans and the variety of sources of finance. Theoretical models of labour-management suggest that two difficulties may be restriction of output to maintain income and a favouring of consumption at the expense of investment. Yugoslavia's experience shows that these pitfalls can be avoided, for industrial production has grown at a rapid rate between 5% and 15% per annum. However, the pace of price increases has been among the greatest outside South America. In practice, control of inflation proved the most intractable problem facing the Yugoslavian labour-managed economy.

CONCLUSION

An extension of workers' control requires the existence of established channels of communication between workers and their representatives; trade union organisation is the most obvious of such channels, although its use in this way depends upon improved standards of accountability. The desirability of a shift in power towards workers, to the extent that they can veto decisions affecting the process of production, is controversial in contemporary political culture. However, all socialists today advocate some form of workers' control although they differ substantially over how it should be exercised. Syndicalists and Guild Socialists are largely responsible for implanting this concept within radical political economy. The Syndicalists emphasised the role of trade unions in promoting social transformation, while the Guild Socialists analysed the institutional structures necessary to achieve, and then maintain, workers' control of industry. The ideas of each gained considerable popularity before and immediately after the First World War, but subsequently fell into decline under the impact of the depression and the failure of strike activity to yield immediate, tangible gains. In recent years the apparent inability of centralised government policies in mixed economies to alter the distribution of power and wealth in favour of the working class has led to renewed interest in Syndicalist and Guild Socialist ideas. More analysis of the ultimate goal, along with detailed consideration of the practical problems, is required, but the fundamental issues — and the ethical challenge underlying them — raised by the concept of workers' control are likely to remain in the forefront of radical economics, and of general political debate, in the years that lie ahead.

NOTES

1 The Knights of Labour was an umbrella organisation for all types of reformers. At their 1880s peak it secured a membership of around 700,000.
2 The military analogies are noteworthy.
3 G. D. H. Cole was its most effective exponent, followed by such as Orage, Penty and S. G. Hobson.
4 Such a perspective contrasts sharply with capitalists' views of their management function, which they typically define as directing and controlling the labour force. The rules governing production processes, workers' behaviour and discipline are determined by a series of capitalist decisions backed by a system of sanctions and penalties. Their vision of firms as unitary structures moving towards a common objective serves three functions as a management ideology; as a method of self-reassurance, an instrument of persuasion and a technique of legitimating authority. If capitalist industry is a harmony of cooperation that only fools or knaves disrupt, owners' confidence is maintained, workers or the public may be convinced and legitimacy is conferred on it. Capitalist discipline becomes acceptable if the interests of managers and managed are identical.
5 Exemplified by the remark of Keynes (1936) that 'consumption is the sole maximand of economic activity'.
6 Matthews (1971) documented its history.
7 In this situation any conceivable reallocation could only increase one individual's welfare at the cost of reducing the welfare of at least one other.

8 Neoclassical Critiques of Capitalism

During the 1870s a type of economic theory known today as neoclassical thought became the orthodoxy among non-Marxists. Its roots stretch back to certain aspects of Adam Smith's (1776) work and the Origin of Profits controversy during the 1830s, but its most influential formulations in Britain were those of Jevons (1871) and Marshall (1890). Neoclassicals concentrated upon microeconomics, applying marginalist concepts to the operation of competitive markets. This application was suceptible to extensive mathematical refinement, which occupied many economists over succeeding generations. The new orthodoxy analysed an economy where:

(i) market choices by consumers are determined by a coherent subjective preference ordering,

(ii) decisions concerning what and how to produce are governed by the desire of suppliers to maximise profit,

(iii) buyers and sellers in total form a market so large that no individual can influence prices through their own actions.

The theory is designed to explain the behaviour of consumers and firms in a more or less competitive environment, where the forces of supply and demand create a unique equilibrium price structure at which the quantities demanded and supplied are equalised so that markets are cleared. From certain axioms concerning the nature of consumer preference orderings and the technical relationship between inputs and outputs, a consistent chain of deductive reasoning leads to the conclusion that a competitive capitalist economy allocates its resources so that no change in production, consumption or distribution could leave one person or group in a preferred position without leaving another in a less preferred position. Consequently resources are efficiently allocated because, given existing tastes and income distribution, it is impossible to increase aggregate output through reallocation.[1] Many neoclassicals argue that scientific objectivity prevents any choice between outcomes that improve the position of one person or class at the expense of another. A competitive capitalist economy appears to satisfy the criterion of 'economic efficiency' since no other system can be shown on objective grounds to represent an improvement. By extending the application of these basic concepts, neoclassicals evolved a distinct policy outlook which stressed the significance of the pursuit of individual self-interest in markets free from government intervention for promoting the well-being of all. However, a number of radical critiques of capitalism have developed from within the neoclassical paradigm.

GENERAL EQUILIBRIUM, 'WAITING' AND EXPLOITATION

Lange (1935) published a theory of capitalist exploitation utilising neoclassical analysis, which is astonishing in its simplicity and whose fundamentals were recently endorsed by such eminent non-radicals as Samuelson (1971) and Lerner (1972). Lange starts his argument from the institutional specification that workers do not own the means of production, which are the exclusive property of a separate capitalist class. He then adds the definitional propositions that this is not as it *should* be (from the normative standpoint of socialist ethics) nor as it *could* be (factually). It follows directly that if profits are positive at long-run equilibrium, workers are exploited *because* they own no capital by those who do. Lange argues that long-run equilibrium profits are positive because:

(i) technical progress is necessary to maintain the capitalist system,

(ii) technical progress takes the form of a 'constant increase in the organic composition of capital,'

(iii) a rising organic composition of capital involves the replacement of workers by machines.

Therefore the industrial reserve army of labour is constantly replenished and wages are prevented from swallowing up profits.

Lange emphasises that this argument does not depend upon any definition of exploitation in terms of a 'surplus' produced by workers which is appropriated by capitalists. It is compatible with any notion of capital (*e.g.* as a supply of waiting) and of profit (*e.g.* as a reward for waiting), while it can be integrated with any otherwise satisfactory theories of relative prices and distribution. Capitalists exploit workers by implicitly denying them the ability to wait and thus to own the means of production they use. Lange's theory is a supreme analytical achievement, and demonstrates how acceptance of neoclassical theories of value, capital and distribution can be compatible with a critique of capitalism.

However, few radical economists in the 1980s see neoclassical equilibrium theory as an impeccable foundation for analysis of either capitalism's operation or capitalist exploitation under competitive conditions. Doubts arise concerning proofs of the existence of general equilibrium and of convergence towards it. Walras (1954) in the seminal presentation of such models postulated tatonnement as the equilibrating process, but this solution rests on the assumption that exchanges take place only at market clearing prices. It does not work effectively when recognised dealers operate by setting their own prices and then wait for others to transact business with them. Before the Walrasian model can be accepted, economists must be satisfied that it has no serious consistency problems. The modern critique of neoclassical capital theory poses the question of whether a Walrasian system (as accepted by Lange) can be in full equilibrium[2] unless it treats capital as a single, perfectly malleable object. Since the unreality of an assumption of malleable capital is beyond dispute, this is a consistency problem of considerable magnitude.[3] Nevertheless Lange's theory indicates that an unequal distribution of income and wealth causes varying abilities to wait, so that individuals undertake market transactions from different initial positions and under different financial presssures. Consequently individual behaviour depends upon the amount of property owned. Without any overt exercise of power, unequal initial positions lead to unequal results for market agents.

MONOPOLY, MONOPSONY AND DISCRIMINATION

A number of theories of capitalist exploitation derive from the empirical observation that perfect competition rarely exists in advanced industrial capitalism, which is characterised by a variety of market structures embodying degrees of monopoly and monopsony. Models of imperfect competition sprang from this observation and became related to various concepts of exploitation. The definitional assumption of Pigou (1920) and Robinson (1933) was the value judgment that exploitation occurs whenever the unit price of a factor of production is less than the value of its marginal physical product; for Chamberlin (1933) exploitation involves a payment below the value of a factor's marginal revenue product.

These statements suffer severe deficiencies as the bases for exploitation theory. They contain no reason why the exploitation rate should be positive at long-run equilibrium, while the value judgements embedded within them are arbitrary and general, so that they become almost impossible to interpret as theories of monopoly capitalist exploitation despite their apparent 'realism'. These value judgements are not unanimously acceptable on ethical grounds; if unit prices of factors are equal to the value of marginal physical products, with no exploitation in the Pigovian sense, the ethical validity of the marginal productivity mode of distribution is not irrefutably proved. Lerner (1939) argued that Pigou's definition sanctions what may be ethically objectionable, for example to each according to its marginal product when the latter derives from environmental and social class differences, or income inequality favouring the privileged in a socialist society with no private property in the means of production.

These theories regard exploitation solely as an outcome of monopolistic and monopsonistic structures in either a capitalist or a socialist economy. On this basis workers, landlords or capitalists could in principle be the victims of exploitation as illustrated by Robinson's standard discussion: 'In so far as labour is strongly organised in trade unions while the supply of land in a particular industry is often perfectly elastic, it is probable that land is more exploitable than labour'. General monopoly definitions of exploitation can only be interpreted as being undertaken unambiguously by, and benefitting, capitalists in terms of the empirical evidence, as Robinson tried to do — 'but the factor of production which is at once the poorest and the most exploitable is unorganised unskilled labour'. Such attempts are theoretically insubstantial since they combine two definitions of exploitation with little direct relation to each other; monopoly and one stating that, whenever inequality exists, the richer are exploiting the poorer. Moreover, even if unskilled workers are identified as the most exploited class, it could be argued on the maximin rule of Rawls (1972) that 'for equal welfare of the worst-off individuals, the second worst-off indivuals etc ... maximise the welfare of the best-off' (*i.e.* the monopoly capitalists). Nor will the alternative 'make the worst-off best-off' criterion necessarily reduce exploitation defined in terms of income inequality.

Therefore monopoly theories of exploitation are in themselves neutral in the struggle between capital and labour, although the general significance of monopoly has been accentuated by the existence of multinational corporations, transfer pricing and modern techniques for manipulating market operations. A crucial feature of monopoly and monopsony power is the possibility it affords of discrimination on such grounds as race, religion and sex. Defenders of capitalism explain this phenomenon in one of two ways. The more reactionary argue that job discrimination reflects the innate inferiority of blacks and women, but the commonest contention is that racism and sexism are products of a fairly universal human bigotry and are not specifically related to capitalism. However, radicals point out that the wages of blacks and women comprise a substantial portion of total costs and so exert a significant impact on profits; thus in 1970 the salaries and wages of women in the United States averaged 42% less than those of men doing the same job, which implies that approximately 23% of manufacturing profits that year were attributable to the lower pay received by women.

Baran and Sweezy (1966) analysed the ways in which capitalists benefit from the existence of a Negro subproletariat:

(i) Employers benefit from divisions in the labour force which enable them to play off one group against another, thus weakening each while impeding the development of effective trade unions.

(ii) Owners of inner-city housing are able to overcrowd and overcharge.

(iii) Middle and upper income groups gain from having a large supply of cheap domestic labour at their disposal.

(iv) Many small businesses can operate profitably only if cheap labour is available.

(v) The existence of lower-paid black labour boosts monopsony profits[4] in many firms.

(vi) Discrimination increases social stability, because each group can compensate for its feelings of inferiority and envy toward those above by feelings of superiority and contempt for those below.

(vii) Racism transfers many whites' perception of the source of their problems from capitalism towards blacks.

(viii) Racism makes it easier to justify the maintenance of an unemployed reserve of black labour for use in booms, which exerts a continual downward pressure on the wages paid to those in work.

Although these assertions pertain to racism, sexism performs similar functions. Most radicals do not believe that capitalism creates these phenomena, but rather that it perpetuates them because they serve its needs. Capitalists benefit both materially and in other ways from racism and sexism, while workers as a whole lose.

UTILITY THEORY AND EGALITARIANISM

Traditional welfare economics, associated with Marshall (1890) and Pigou (1920), included a case for income equalisation based upon two propositions:

(i) The utility functions of all individuals are cardinally measurable with continuous first derivatives, from which negatively inclined marginal utility curves for income can be derived.

(ii) The utility schedules of any two individuals are comparable, either because they are to a sufficient approximation identical, or because their differences themselves reflect inequalities of background.

The logical consequence of these propositions is the complete equalisation of incomes to maximise total utility.

At first glance the notion of declining marginal utility of income appears to justify the adoption of progressive taxation, but such a conclusion does not inevitably follow. If all individuals with the same income possess an identical capacity for satisfying wants so that the schedule relating income and utility is the same for all taxpayers and if the government seeks to distribute its tax bill to achieve 'equal sacrifice' in terms of surrendered income, the optimal tax structure depends on the definition of 'equal sacrifice'. There are three possibilities:

(i) equal *absolute* sacrifice, *i.e.* a distribution of the tax bill which extracts the same absolute amount of income-utility from each individual,

(ii) equal *proportional* sacrifice, *i.e.* the extraction of the same proportion of total income-utility from each individual,

(iii) equal *marginal* sacrifice, *i.e.* the minimisation of aggregate sacrifice by imposing an identical marginal sacrifice of income-utility upon each individual.

It is unclear on a priori ground which of these definitions should be chosen, but in all cases the actual tax structure required to implement 'equal sacrifice' depends on the precise shape of the income-utility curve. If all that is known is that the marginal utility of income declines at some undetermined speed over its entire range, progression is only justified by adopting the concept of equal marginal sacrifice under which the highest income is levelled by tax down to the level of the next highest, and so on, until the necessary revenue is raised.

Other problems arise in attempting to advocate progressive taxation by utility theory. Even if the marginal utility of income declines at a given income level, an increase in income may cause the schedule to shift upwards as individual aspirations rise. When the long-run path connecting the points on the upward shifting short-term schedules is constant, none of the three concepts supports a progressive tax structure, while the achievement of equal absolute sacrifice requires regressive taxation. Further complications arise when individuals' utility schedules are interdependent, so that satisfaction is derived not from one's own income but one's place in the distributive hierarchy. The egalitarian tax case rests on the assumption that redistribution does not cause a movement in the position of individual marginal utility schedules, which is unlikely, as the policy proposals arousing controversy are of a magnitude which makes the application of marginal analysis questionable. Moreover, differences in tastes, and thus in the trade-off between income and utility, prevent the derivation of any conclusions about the optimum tax rate structure from concepts of equal sacrifice unless interpersonal comparisons of utility are made. If it be admitted that individuals vary in their capacity for want satisfaction, governments should seek to produce larger incomes for the most efficient utility engines if these could be distinguished. It has been argued that, in the absence of specific knowledge, equal capacities for satisfaction should be assumed, but identical income-utility curves are no more plausible than different ones, since each possibility has a 50% chance of occurring. Once variations in income-utility functions are allowed, any distribution can be justified by inferring differing capacities for satisfaction from observed income itself.

The optimum tax structure cannot be determined in isolation. Even if the notion of a monotonically declining marginal utility of income is accepted, a proportional or regressive income tax could be advocated providing that government expenditure largely benefits the poor. The effectiveness of any redistribution depends upon whether it is achieved through tax or expenditure changes, since it is difficult to believe that individual marginal utility of income schedules are independent, in either position or slope, of the manner in which income is acquired or lost. Therefore, in terms of utility theory, Edgeworth's (1877) denial of the widespread belief that decreasing marginal utility of income is all that is necessary in order to deduce progressiveness of taxation from the postulate of equal sacrifice seems difficult to refute. Certainly contemporary welfare economics confines itself, on principle, to propositions that can be established without the aid of either interpersonal comparisons or measurement of utility. The main result is to deprive many egalitarian propositions of their neoclassical foundations, because attempts to derive maldistribution conclusions from utility analysis end in failure unless they involve implicitly or explicitly the questionable comparability and measurability assumptions. Without these, a preference for one distribution over another can be derived from neoclassical theory only by inserting it into initial assumptions.

LIMITATIONS OF THE NEOCLASSICAL MARKET PARADIGM

The effectiveness of the analyses discussed in this chapter ultimately rests on the validity of the neoclassical paradigm from which they derive, with its emphasis on the pursuit of individual self-interest in markets free from government control. Such a paradigm is based, despite numerous qualifications, upon the model of perfect competition in which rational consumers indicate their preferences to profit-maximising producers through the medium of price. However, radicals have devoted considerable attention to the limitations of the neoclassical model, and contemporary welfare theorists accept that the market behaviour of individuals is unlikely to generate the norm of ideal output[5] if certain market failures occur. The principal acknowledged market failures are as follows:

(i) Orthodox economists accept as given the preferences of individual consumers, yet are trapped in tautology as preferences can only be deduced from actual patterns of expenditure. Their models determine a price-output equilibrium only when supply and demand are independent; autonomous shifts in demand are seen as generating, via price and profit movements, appropriate changes in production in the same direction. However, individual preferences are increasingly formulated after exposure to the actions of those satisfying them. The process of creating wants, exemplified by the outlay on advertising and market research, may or may not yield gains for specific participating firms but in total it can affect consumers' behaviour. To the extent that this occurs, there is no meaningful way in which industry can be said to meet demand, since the latter cannot be identified until the volume and intensity of sales effort is specified. If advertising were purely informative, it would enable more knowledgable pursuit of a fixed set of preferences, but almost inevitably it generates changes in the preferences themselves. In these circumstances, rather than producers responding to exogenous shifts in demand, they create endogenous movements[6] which they then proceed to satisfy.

(ii) Some buyers and sellers are sufficiently large to affect prices by their actions. The character of modern productive techniques and the associated economies of scale have made monopolistic and monopsonistic markets more frequent. Monopoly tends to keep prices higher and outputs lower than those prevailing under competition. A series of influences, such as the minimum scale of efficient production, the urge for market control, advertising and inflation, protect large corporations to a considerable extent from market forces. Consequently the antithesis frequently drawn between public and private enterprise (the former inefficient and bureaucratic; the latter efficient and purposeful) is outmoded since the presence of monopoly elements implies that production is rarely extended to the point of Pareto optimality.

(iii) Some commodities are consumed socially, so their production and sale can never be profitable in an economy based solely upon individual market behaviour, even though they may be considered desirable by most citizens. 'Pure' public goods are defined as those which cannot be consumed individually (*e.g.* museums, art galleries, concert halls, police, defence) or those which have to be made available to many if they are available to some because their effects are global and cannot easily be localised (*e.g.* roads, lighthouses, flood control, sewage, water). Consumption of these goods and services by one person in no way reduces the consumption opportunities of others, while people who do not pay for them cannot be excluded from the resulting benefits, so that no market mechanism can reveal the optimum level of provision or its method of finance. These issues must be resolved through some communal political process.

(iv) External economies occur whenever the private costs or benefits from production diverge from the costs and benefits to society. Where the costs of a commodity to the producer are lower than its social costs, it is possible that for society costs exceed benefits even though profits are made; environmental pollution and road congestion are frequently cited examples. Conversely some commodities (for example certain types of education and medical care) generate social benefits that are not taken into account by individual consumers and producers. In these cases price does not reflect the benefit of consuming the marginal unit, and marginal cost does not measure the opportunity cost of producing it. A variety of methods for dealing with externalities can be devised, such as bargaining between the parties involved, prohibition, enforcement of compensation, litigation and the imposition of a tax or payment of a subsidy, but each involves manipulation of the price mechanism before it can achieve a desired outcome. External economies therefore present a challenge to market allocation of resources.

(v) Consumer preferences are represented in the market only to the extent that they are supported by purchasing power. An infinite number of Pareto optima exist, each involving a different distribution of income and wealth, between which no comparisons can be drawn without making value judgements about 'fairness'. Neoclassical analysis separates the normative issue of distributive justice from the positive analysis of market efficiency, but ignoring the corrections between distribution and allocation is unrealistic. It is impossible to develop comprehensive norms for resource allocation independent of the distribution of income, which affects desired patterns of consumption and hence welfare; thus status symbols and material emulation in general may figure less prominently in a society with greater equality. It is impossible to derive an objective means of choosing amongst distributions. Each society adopts some target and devises policies to reach it. Rawls (1972) suggested three principles that could furnish distributive criteria:

(a) Each person engaged in or affected by an activity has an equal right to the most extensive liberty compatible with a like liberty for all.

(b) No inequality is just unless it is to the advantage of the most unfortunate individual, *i.e.* inequalities must work to everyone's advantage.

(c) Inequalities deriving from positions and offices held in society should be equally accessible to the competition of all on the basis of their ability.

These principles do not prescribe a uniquely just distribution of income or any particular pattern of resource ownership. Rawls seeks to maximise the benefit of the least advantaged, a criterion which falls short of total equality but which would require a large state apparatus to implement, since markets tend to recreate and reinforce inequality.

(vi) On occasions individuals' preferences diverge so substantially from their welfare as perceived by others that governments feel justified in overruling market outcomes. Fear of totalitarianism creates a widespread desire to reduce the area of intervention but few argue that it can be eliminated completely, for example, in the affairs of children, drug addicts, criminals and the mentally sick.[7] Therefore the crucially unresolved issue becomes establishing political criteria to determine where the line between market adaptations to individual demand and state regulation should be drawn.

(vii) The efficiency of market operations is justified by neoclassicals in terms of the adjustment of the structure of production to consumers' preferences. However, such adjustments occur after a time lag, for supply is only increased if a higher level of demand persists for a sufficient length of time to ensure profitability. These delays are unimportant for many commodities, but can be crucial in the case of necessities where government intervention to raise production quickly may be required (*e.g.* basic foodstuffs, fuels, drugs, armaments in wartime).

(viii) Some productive resources are unique and non-sustainable. If the possibility exists that they may become exhausted within a foreseeable timespan (*e.g.* coal, oil) a market mechanism responding exclusively to short-term financial considerations is unlikely to protect the interests of future generations. Contemporary examples are: (a) the conversion of fertile agricultural land into dust bowls by maximising immediate profits; (b) fears that the virtual disappearance of tropical rain forests by the end of the twentieth century on current rates of depletion may upset the earth's ecological balance.

(ix) Uncontrolled market economies have historically been subject to recurring depressions that involve heavy social and economic costs. One reason is the uncertainty that surrounds investment decisions, which magnifies the other causes of market failure and leads to cyclical instability. In an individualistic economy uncertainty plays an active rather than a passive role; Keynes (1936) argued that expenditure on investment is the crucial factor determining output and employment and that it depends to a considerable extent on the anticipation of profits. Since these anticipations are notoriously volatile, capitalist growth is likely to be erractic. Moreover, no automatic mechanism exists to ensure that planned investment is sufficient to secure full employment, so that Keynes looked to the state to manipulate aggregate demand for achieving this objective and the associated promise of economic growth.

Most neoclassicals accept that when any of these market failures occur they can be corrected only by government intervention. They differ concerning the practical importance of this observation, but their concentration upon market analysis implies that failures constitute essentially minor exceptions capable of correction by an enlightened state. In practice, however, the demands placed upon governments would be considerable; for instance, the range of external benefits and costs is large in an urbanised industrial economy. The theoretical case for state control to make markets more efficient was greatly extended by the work of Pigou (1920) at the micro, and Keynes (1936) at the macro, level of analysis.

These statements concerning potential causes of market failure are located within the neoclassical framework, yet even more serious criticism of this overall paradigm can be made once it is rigorously developed and its full implications perceived. Its assumptions do not correspond even remotely to reality; thus de Graff (1957) formulated a comprehensive list of seventeen restrictive assumptions, *each* of which must be fulfilled before a market mechanism can achieve the Pareto optimum allocation of resources. These include the implausible assumptions that:

(i) each indivual's welfare is identical with their preference ordering, *i.e.* that children, criminals, drug addicts and the insane, as well as all others, always prefer what is best for them,

(ii) neither risk nor uncertainty is ever present,

(iii) productivity is totally unaffected by the existing distribution of wealth,

(iv) all capital and consumer goods are infinitely divisible.

These represent but four of the essential conditions, all of which must be realised before the market can achieve an optimum allocation of resources. Some of the phenomena that neoclassical theory ignores should also be noted; among the more important are collective aspirations and the dependence of the structure of demand on a particular social milieu. Moreover, as the community is composed of one set of persons at one time and another at another time, it is difficult to state if and when the community is better off. De Graff commented that 'the measure of acceptance this theory has won among professional economists would be astonishing were not its pedigree so long and respectable'.

Given the implausibility of these assumptions it is obvious that Pareto optimality can never be more than a normative model towards which governments might attempt to move a capitalist economy. The goal itself could not possibly be achieved. Even such partial arguments for locating the Pareto optimum founder against the 'Theory of the Second Best' developed by Lipsey and Lancaster (1956-7). This theory states, on the basis of a mathematical proof, that in situations characterised by any deviation from perfect optimality, partial policy measures which eliminate only some of the causes of market failure may create a net decline in welfare. Therefore government endeavours to improve the operation of free markets may produce opposite effects to those intended. Moving towards the optimum is insufficient; if it cannot be attained, conventional criteria provide no guidelines for choosing between available alternatives. Since all models with possible relevance for policy inevitably relate to second best situations, the implications of this theory for the neoclassical paradigm are devastating.

Moreover, Arrow (1963) demonstrated that if consumer sovereignty is adopted as a fundamental criterion while interpersonal comparisons of welfare are simultaneously denied (two of the basic tenets of orthodox economics), any coherent programme of government action must be imposed upon citizens. No type of democratic voting under these two basic assumptions can be shown to yield a consistently ordered set of alternatives for the guidance of policy-makers. State measures take on an ad hoc nature whereby the gainers and losers are identified and the merits of their respective claims evaluated in terms of efficiency, equity and the variety of goals a government is pursuing. Significantly these developments occurred within the mainstream of neoclassical economics, whose ideology pushed to its logical conclusion destroys its own foundations.

CONCLUSION

The neoclassical paradigm, with its stress on marginalist concepts to explain how markets work, has sometimes been used explicitly, but more frequently implicitly, to establish the market mechanism as the normal method of resource allocation and to justify its use on the grounds of its efficiency in meeting consumer preferences. However, a number of critiques of capitalism have been mounted from within the framework of neoclassical theory. The most important of these, for example: workers' inability to wait, the prevalence of monopoly and the possible egalitarian implications of utility theory, focus upon phenomena that are of considerable significance in any radical worldview, but the weaknesses inherent in the neoclassical paradigm render it at best a limited tool for analysing the nature of exploitation in a capitalist economy. These limitations of economic orthodoxy have provided a crucial stimulant to the revival of radical political economy in western countries since the early 1960s.

NOTES

1 This situation is usually termed the 'Pareto optimum' in honour of Pareto, its first formulator. The 'Pareto optimum' is defined as an allocation of resources such that no one's welfare can be improved without harming someone else, while a 'Pareto improvement' involves raising one person's welfare without harming anyone else. 'Welfare' in this context means what a person prefers according to their own standards, so that it involves intrapersonal (but not interpersonal) comparisons.
2 Nuti (1970) pointed out that full employment implies (a) equality of the net rates of return on all kinds of capital goods, with the price of the latter equal to their cost of production, as well as (b) the equality of the net rates of return on capital goods and the quantities of new capital goods currently produced.
3 Chapter Ten discusses the 'Capital Controversy' in greater detail.
4 Burkitt (1980) analysed the operation of monopsonistic market structures.
5 Pigou (1920) defined ideal output as a combination of commodities such that 'no alternative output which could be obtained by reallocation of the economy's resources would leave the community better off than before'.
6 Planned obsolescene, the addition of unnecessary frills and packaging, and the introduction of new products are all methods of achieving this objective.
7 This principle can be applied to a wider range of activities; thus few advocate the purchase and sale of firearms on a commercial basis, unless subject to government regulation.

9 Schumpeter's Theory of the Advent of Socialism

'Capitalism will be destroyed by its success not its failure ... Its very success undermines the social institutions which protect it and inevitably creates conditions in which it will not be able to live and strongly point to socialism as its heir apparent'.

J. A. Schumpeter, 1942

In *Capitalism, Socialism and Democracy*, published in 1942, Schumpeter put forward a unique economic hypothesis. Most of those who anticipate the replacement of capitalism by socialism advocate such a development, but Schumpeter had little love for socialism and none for socialists; his nature sympathies belong to the heroic age of expanding capitalism. Nonetheless he regards capitalism as doomed and socialism as inevitable for the apparently paradoxical reason that the success of capitalist economies destroys them and creates the conditions for socialism to emerge as the dominant mode of production.

SCHUMPETER'S THEORY OF CAPITALIST BREAKDOWN

Schumpeter provides a number of reasons for believing that capitalism will break down and be replaced by socialism:

(i) Capitalists' achievements in developing productive capccity which creates a higher standard of living for all classes, undermine their social and political position, as their economic function, although not obsolete, tends to become obsolescent and amenable to bureaucratisation. Schumpeter sees capitalism as a system of change, a gale of creative destruction, characterised over time by the emergence of new commodities, techniques of production, markets, forms of transport and industrial organisation. From this perspective even monopolies face competition over time when the activity of entrepreneurs brings about an ever-shifting pattern of market advantages. The basic role of the entrepreneur is to innovate, which involves not the scientific activity of invention but overcoming environmental resistance to change, thus getting things done. Initiating novel commodities and production techniques is a difficult task which constitutes a distinct economic function.

The role of the entrepreneur declines as capitalism matures. Innovation becomes less the preserve of individuals and increasingly the routine impersonalised function of teams of corporate officials rewarded by salaries rather than profits for their collective activity. They could perform this role equally well, after initial shock, in nationalised industries. Indeed the bureaucratic structure of both private and public large corporations is not dissimilar. Therefore the success of capitalism in automating technical progress (through research teams and corporate activity) leads to the erosion of the capitalists' essential function. Moreover, due to economies of scale larger firms tend to drive the smaller and less efficient out of business so hastening the mechanisation of innovation to the detriment of entrepreneurship. Resistance to change lessens as change itself, in the form of a stream of new producer and consumer goods, becomes customary. As the capitalists' innovative role becomes performed by collective methods, the link between innovation and financial self-interest is broken and the economic basis of the bourgeoisie, rendered superfluous by its own success, is reduced to wages for administration.

Three groups are primarily involved in the direction of large modern capitalist enterprises:

(a) salaried managers, who tend to adopt the attitudes of employees and not to identify closely with shareholders' interests,

(b) large institutional shareholders, which are concerned with corporate success but are not in a position to exercise the functions of individual proprietors,

(c) small shareholders, who are remote from managerial influence and may be hostile to big business.

None of these has the capacity or the desire to fulfil the capitalist's former role. In Schumpeter's words 'the pacemakers of socialism are not Marx and his followers but Carnegie, Rockefeller and Vanderbilt'. It is much easier, economically, politcally and administratively, to socialise a few large plants than numerous small ones. Nationalisation of the local fish and chip shop removes the incentive to efficiency from the proprietors, but no such effect upon the 'owners' of a multinational corporation is likely. Therefore every increase in average firm size prepares the way for the potential socialisation of private business.

As a result of these developments, a growing indifference to the institutions of capitalism is likely to prove fatal to them in the long run.[1] The material substance of property becomes defunctionalised by absentee ownership which fails to call forth allegiance. The elimination of small-scale entrepreneurs removes the social base of bourgeois democracy. In the middle of the nineteenth century around 80% of the U.S. labour force owned the means of production with which they worked. A century later approximately the same proportion consisted of wage and salary earners. Their living standards as consumers had risen, but their social status changed with the gradual extinction of the private entrepreneur as the mainspring of economic activity.

(ii) Schumpeter contends that capitalist activity is essentially 'rational', spreading habits of mind which destroy the loyalties of super- and sub-ordination essential for acceptance of the institutionalised leadership of production units. No social system can operate effectively which is based exclusively upon a network of free contracts between legally equal parties each guided solely by their own self-interest. The philosophy and practice of Keynesianism, which appeared between 1940 and the mid-1970s to offer permanent full employment, plays a crucial role in accentuating this problem. Depressions are not simply accidental blemishes in the course of capitalism's development but fulfil functions central to its existence; the associated bankruptcies, rationalisations and take-over bids help eliminate inefficient enterprises, while the continual threat and periodic ocurrence of mass unemployment exerts a dual effect—it inhibits workers from pressing inflationary wage claims[2] and maintains the industrial discipline imposed by capital upon labour within the factory. The threat of dismissal has always been the most potent sanction underpinning factory rules and regulations. Many of the contemporary problems faced by capitalist economies derive from the loosening of some of the constraints faced by the working class during the period of continuous full employment between 1940 and 1970.[3]

(iii) The concentration of capitalists upon the workplace is instrumental in creating a political system and a class structure which contain social groups that under certain circumstances may be indifferent, and under others hostile, to the fundamental institutions of private enterprise. If capitalism is to break down, some interests must exist which encourage and organise resentment against it. Schumpeter believes that capitalist economies are unique in sponsoring influential groups with potential motives for unrest against the status quo. These include:

(a) *the industrial working class*, which could develop the power (as it forms a majority), the interest (because capitalism provides it with a subordinate economic and social position) and the capability to transform society in the direction of socialism (through trade unions and other organisations). Ultimately workers' alienation may stimulate 'radical needs' whose satisfaction requires a qualitatively different social structure.[4]

(b) *a political sector* composed of elected politicians and administrators. This develops under capitalist democracy, because the political and economic decision-takers remain distinct in contrast to the preceding feudal system. Business leadership is unglamorous, enjoying none of the prestige accorded—even to some extent today—to the aristocracy. Schumpeter argues that the political sector's attitude to private enterprise underwent a gradual yet fundamental change in the twentieth century, with the result that it initiates raids against profits through its budgetary and other policies that prove lucrative in the short run to other classes.

(c) *intellectuals*, defined as those who wield the power of the written or spoken word, yet are not directly responsible for practical affairs. Schumpeter believes that they possess a vested interest in social unrest because:

(1) they are invariably critical, so that their attacks on individual capitalists and institutions gradually undermine the status quo. Moreover, their criticisms become effective across a larger audience with universal education and the growth of mass communications;

(2) expansion in student numbers produces more highly educated workers than can be absorbed into jobs consistent with their expectations, so that a growing group of discontented intellectuals emerges;

(3) intellectuals participate in politics and provide theories, facts and statistics which strengthen the labour movement. Due

to their divergent social background, they tend to become left militants, thus transforming the character of trade unions and working-class parties.

(iv) Schumpeter argues that these factors loosen the hold of capitalist values upon the public and even over capitalists themselves, so that public policy grows more antagonistic to business interests and often refuses on principle to take them into account. Profit maximisation is impeded by the development of 'modern populism'; *i.e.* desires for general economic management, environmental improvement, recognition and security provide an increasingly hostile atmosphere in which capitalists will eventually cease to function. Their most glamorous ambition, to found an industrial dynasty, is already unattainable in most countries, while the scope for entrepreneurial activity reduces as innovation becomes routine.

(v) Schumpeter believes that capitalist evolution disintegrates the bourgeois family. The large bourgeois family typical of early capitalism sought to establish and maintain an industrial dynasty, an objective obliging it to look to the long run with saving and reinvestment as instruments to build up family businesses for future generations. The possibility of establishing a family dynasty becomes increasingly remote with the development of large corporations enjoying cost advantages due to economies of scale. Consequently parents take a different attitude to childbearing, weighing the benefits and costs of parenthood, so that familial as well as economic behaviour becomes rationalised. In early capitalism the balance of advantage was almost universally considered to rest on the side of large families, but as the system matures prevailing attitudes shift towards having a small number of children. This decline in the family's importance reduces the centrality of entrepreneurial struggles to provide for subsequent generations, so that the capitalist mentality further erodes.

(vi) To demonstrate how far the disintegration of capitalism had proceeded by the 1940s, Schumpeter lists the following policies which capitalist governments frequently resorted to:

(a) stabilisation measures to prevent recessions, *e.g.* aggregate demand management to preserve full employment;

(b) redistributive taxation to promote greater equality;

(c) regulation of price levels through such measures as monopoly control and incomes policies;

(d) extension of public enterprise;

(e) detailed control of both the labour and the financial markets;

(f) welfare provisions designed to mitigate the insecurity placed upon individuals by the operation of an unregulated economy.

Not all these policies can be labelled 'socialist', but their prevalence indicates the extent to which capitalism has evolved from *laissez faire* as governments seek to regulate the operation and outcome of capitalist institutions. Moreover, the remedy for unsuccessful intervention is seen as more rather than less state activity, while many who oppose socialism and deny the existence of any tendency towards it unquestionably accept interventionist measures. For Schumpter the essence of capitalism lies not merely in individual choice of products, processes and jobs, but in a scheme of values, an attitude to life and the civilisation of inequality which is passing away. He illustrated the existence of this trend by pointing to the failure of capitalist solutions to work in the contemporary economic environment—for example, the problems created by Britain's inter-war policies; in a world that was no longer one of untrammelled free enterprise, the gold standard[5] produced unacceptable results. Capitalists become afraid of the adjustments involved in applying market policies and accept the imposition of fiscal burdens which would have been considered intolerable in earlier periods.

The state extracts by taxation and other economic policies much of what nineteenth-century socialists termed 'surplus value'. Businesss cannot maximise profits when its most important parameters (*e.g.* prices, wages and interest) are determined by elected politicians or bureaucrats. Schumpeter believes that capitalism would stagnate if private enterprise continued to be regulated and taxed at the 1940s level, in which case socialism may then seem to be the lesser evil even to its enemies.

Consequently Schumpeter argues that socialism is inevitable if defined as an economy where the means of production, decisions on what and how to produce and distribution are controlled by public authority rather than privately-owned firms. Migration of economic affairs from the private to the public sphere inevitably entails a large bureaucracy.

THE ROLE OF INFLATION IN THE TRANSITION TO SOCIALISM

One of the factors accelerating economic and social changes is inflation. Schumpeter contends that rising prices are prevalent when all are afraid of the short-run consequences of anti-inflationary policy and when some of the countervailing measures (*e.g.* a fall in real wages) are difficult to achieve. At high levels of employment wage demands become both inevitable (as full employment removes the only reason for not granting them) and inflationary (for when resources are fully utilised, bank borrowing and upward revision of prices provide easy methods of satisfying wage claims). In these circumstances changes in money wage rates no longer affect output and employment but only the value of the monetary unit. This perennial inflationary pressure weakens the social framework, a tendency exacerbated by the standard remedies:

(i) Monetary policy is currently fashionable. Restrictive credit exerts an opposite effect when applied to modern economies than to flexible markets. A higher rate of interest and a lower money supply is supposed to reduce the volume of economic activity, money wages and employment but if such effects materialise, pressures mount for government measures to neutralise them. Therefore the major effect of monetary policy is to increase business difficulties.

(ii) Fiscal policy faces similar problems. Higher taxes have a smaller or even negative effect upon inflation, for if economic growth is to continue, increasing use of bank credit is necessary to overcome any loss in available finance. Increased taxation of wages fuels inflationary claims to maintain real income as do greater indirect tax rates.

(iii) The third alternative, direct controls over prices and incomes, represents a conquest of ground for the bureaucracy, a decisive advance in the conquest of the profit motive by trade unions and the loss of a line of retreat for business (*i.e.* price adjustments when profits fall). Therefore prices and incomes policies involve a surrender of private enterprise to public authority and are a major movement towards the planned economy.

Perennial inflation can play a crucial role in the transition to socialism by assisting the conquest of private industry by bureaucracy. Any resulting frictions may be attributed to capitalist propulsions and so be used to justify further state regulation. Central planning gradually becomes seen as the least possible evil, so that capitalism is no longer worth defending. Inflation normally increases government, at the expense of private, net worth because public agencies possess heavy debts whose burden is steadily reduced by rising prices; for instance, in 1966 total U.K. public debt amounted to approximately 90% of total public assets and public net worth represented only 4½% of national wealth, but by 1975 the increased public debt amounted to only 47% of public assets leaving a public net worth equal to 20% of national wealth. This constitutes a major growth of the public sector, which is likely to continue in mixed economies experiencing inflation.

SCHUMPETER'S STRATEGY FOR SOCIALIST TRANSITION

Schumpeter's vision is Marxist in that he visualises the economic process as socialising itself, so that the administrative, organisational, psychological and technical prerequisites for socialism increasingly become fulfilled. Business is controlled by a small number of large corporations, innovation is collectively planned, industrial property and management is depersonalised, while executives acquire a bureaucratic habit of mind. Progress occurs by slow degrees, so that scope exists at any point in time for divergences of opinion as to whether capitalism is sufficiently mature to permit socialism. Even if an unmistakable state of maturity is reached, transition requires distinct action and presents a series of problems. At the limiting extreme socialism could be adopted as the principle of economic organisation by constitutional amendment, but maturity is more likely to be attained while capitalist interests have not completely vanished. Therefore the passing of constitutional changes is more than a formality, since it provokes resistance to be surmounted. The history of socialisation divides into two stages separated by the act of adopting a socialist economy. Before that act, it is preparatory; after, it is constitutive.

Socialisation after the act only involves the replacement of managers of large-scale concerns for specific reasons. Private partnerships existing at the date of transition are first transformed into corporate structures and then socialised, while the formation of new firms is prohibited. Intercorporate relations are reduced to those securing administrative efficiency, and commercial banks become branch offices of the central planning institutions.

Socialisation before the act occurs when socialists gain political control of the organs of the capitalist state, while institutions and opinions remain unprepared; in particular, a large number of small and medium-sized enterprises still exist. Consequently losses in entrepreneurial energy and productive efficiency follow from a programme of nationalisation, especially when the bureaucracy and organised labour are ill-prepared for such a transformation and possess no structured alternative to the established order. Capital could effectively refuse both assent and cooperation, so that a combination of political opportunity with economic unpreparedness characterises every immature socialisation.

Schumpeter develops a strategy of gradual socialisation within the framework of capitalism, devoting particular attention to Britain where in his view the industrial and commercial structure was not ripe for successful one-stroke socialism as the concentration of corporate control had not proceeded sufficiently far. However, the twentieth century witnessed a slackening in entrepreneurial effort along with a simultaneous growth of state intervention. A socialisation policy incorporating an extensive programme of public ownership was feasible in Britain, while leaving undisturbed for an indefinite time the interests and activities not included within it.

Schumpeter argued in 1942 that the following departments of British industry could be socialised without serious loss of efficiency or major repercussions on other sectors, given that appropriate compensation was paid to their former owners:

(i) The banking apparatus was ripe for nationalisation. The Bank of England had evolved into little more than a Treasury Department, while concentration and bureaucratisation had developed extensively within commercial banking. The large banks could be compelled to absorb the remaining small independents and then be merged with the Bank of England into a National Banking Administration, covering savings banks, building societies and other financial institutions, without any customer being aware of the change outside its media presentation. Scope for greater efficiency exists in coordinating services and increasing government influence over private industry.

(ii) The insurance business was largely mechanised. It could be integrated with state social security, while efficiency gains are available from state control of insurance company funds and a reduction in the cost of selling policies.

(iii) An obvious candidate for state management was transport incorporating civil aviation, railways and road haulage.

(iv) Public ownership would increase efficiency on technical grounds in mining, particularly coal, coal products and tar, although the case could not be extended to chemicals where private enterprise remained active.

(v) The production, transmission and distribution of electric current.

(vi) Iron and steel had 'sown its capitalist wild oats' and could henceforth be administered by the state. Such administration increases productivity through coordination and the establishment of a large research department with little danger of losing entrepreneurial initiative.

(vii) With the possible exception of the architects' role, the building and building materials industries are already regulated and subsidised by the state in a variety of ways, so that net gains could be achieved through coordination by a Public Building Authority.

Schumpeter admitted that this list was not exhaustive, but argued that any additions required justification in 1942 by special, mostly non-economic reasons; armaments, shipbuilding and trade in foodstuffs provided possible examples. He thought that his list was sufficiently comprehensive to keep socialists busy for a considerable time and to induce concessions from them to capitalists, although technical and administrative developments would lead to additional industries becoming ready for socialisation over time. Schumpeter's ideas bear considerable similarity to the post-1945 nationalisation programme undertaken in Britain by the Atlee Government.

SCHUMPETER AND CAPITALIST BREAKDOWN: AN EVALUATION

When evaluating Schumpeter's theory of capitalist breakdown, it must be remembered that he analyses long-run tendencies and regards a century as short term in this context. Consequently no conclusions are possible, only a number of tentative observations:

(i) Capitalism evolved significantly in the last century with the result that innovation became increasingly the product of organised group activity rather than of individual behaviour. However, this development need not necessarily lead to any loss of capitalist vigour, since managers tend to identify with, and be dedicated to fostering, their firms' financial interests due to their own long-term advantage, pride of accomplishment and desire to be associated with a flourishing enterprise. Although managers as distinct from owners play a more crucial role, it is not clear that they form a distinct class nor that their policies are determined by considerations other than profit. Sargant Florence (1953) demonstrated that the number of firms controlled by persons with a negligible shareholding is small, so that decisions on crucial issues are mainly taken by the largest stockholders. Schumpeter's point is valid to the extent that some divorce between ownership and control occurs, while the functions exercised by hired managers could potentially be divorced from the profit motive. This does not imply that in economies operating under capitalist propulsions such potentialities are realised without intense struggle.

(ii) The power of vested corporate interests remain substantial. Their prosperity is vital to the fortunes of national economies so that the state is forced to govern in conformity with their financial requirements unless it undertakes large-scale nationalisation. No government will be re-elected if the rate of profit falls below a certain crucial minimum, because investment would then dry up, business confidence evaporate and living standards fall. Moreover, large corporations maximise profits no less than small firms because of pressures imposed on them by market operation. The relationship between the state and big business was well illustrated in 1975 by the behaviour of the British Labour Government which relaxed price controls and corporate taxation to alleviate the private sector's financial difficulties. Such a policy hardly indicated a socialist desire to use the lack of profitability to extend public ownership. The image of private enterprise benefits from the concentration of nationalisation in declining industries, whose provision of energy, fuel and transport at a loss provides a direct boost to profits. Again Schumpeter pointed to a potentiality rather than an actual occurrence, for it is undoubtedly true that large corporations could perform under different constraints than small-scale units; thus I.C.I. could be nationalised without any inevitable loss of efficiency, whereas the incorporation of a one-person newsagency into the public sector would almost certainly diminish incentive.

(iii) The fall in size of the average bourgeois family need not necessarily inhibit capitalist motivation. Smaller families may result from a desire to enjoy higher consumption per head, more spacious housing, improved education, greater saving and the wish to bequeath an estate.

(iv) In a capitalist democracy economic and political power is formally separated, but in practice both sets of power holders tend to belong to the same class, possess similar privileges and share common assumptions. They have the incentive and the resources to maintain their position and transmit it across generations. Moreover, most governments retain political power under conditions of universal suffrage only if they preside over rising living standards, which depend upon securing a minimum rate of profit and preserving a socio-economic environment which in general conforms to capitalist opinions. In no other way can prosperity be achieved in a largely private enterprise economy. Some manoeuvre for redistribution exists but only within restricted limits.

(v) Intellectuals tend to be critical of the status quo both generally and on specific issues, but their criticism may be constructive and so improve, or help to sustain, capitalism. It could be argued, for instance, that Keynesian economics, with its emphasis on maintaining full employment by manipulating aggregate demand, played such a role after the Second World War. Radical beliefs are held only by a minority of intellectuals, many of whom are employed by private corporations, the government or the communications media owned by capitalists and operated on market principles to disseminate the conventional wisdom.

(vi) As a result of these tendencies, the majority of classes identified by Schumpeter as potentially disaffected (*i.e.* workers, politicians, bureaucrats and intellectuals) have not yet persistently demanded the abolition of capitalism. The media which presents news in a way that propagates capitalist values plays a crucial role in the formation of public opinion. In a technologically advanced economy, the methods of news transmission are so costly that alternatives to capitalist perspectives are rarely ventilated on a large scale. Moreover, the gradual extinction of the individual entrepreneur as the mainspring of the market economy generated more ambiguous consequences than Schumpeter envisaged, for it confronted socialists with a set of new unexpected problems:

(a) the transformation of unregulated into planned capitalism,

(b) the difficulties created by social stratification resting upon differences of status and education,

(c) the unsolved theoretical dilemma of how to relate physical and mental labour.

CONCLUSION

In the years which have elapsed since Schumpeter wrote *Capitalism, Socialism and Democracy*, capitalism has proved durable, with private property remaining strongly entrenched despite the occurrence of many of the trends he envisaged. Government economic interventions increased in scope and volume but remain limited, with the operation of competition still influential. However, Schumpeter's theory of capitalist breakdown applies to the long-term, and new problems for the system are constantly emerging which could threaten its future (*e.g.* multinationals, mergers, stagflation, world migration of capital, new technology, prices and incomes policies) in ways which can be analysed within the framework of Schumpeter's theory. Certainly, although his vision has still to occur, his ideas retain contemporary relevance.

APPENDIX: THE ECONOMIC PHILOSOPHY OF GALBRAITH

The post-war theories of Galbraith (1952, 1958, 1967, 1974) can be interpreted as an extension of Schumpeter's analysis although they incorporate additional considerations. He argues that the success of individual entrepreneurs led to the rise of large corporations in which innovation becomes bureaucratic. Within these corporations the diffusion of stockholding prevents most shareholders from exercising significant decision-making powers, while increased reliance upon internal funding reduces dependence upon external financiers. The size and complexity of modern firms converts top managers into figureheads who approve or veto proposals which evolve from committees manned by middle income specialists, whom Galbraith collectively terms *the technostructure*, currently performing the major proportion of entrepreneurial functions.

Galbraith argues that this development leads to a breakdown of the market mechanism, partly due to increased planning; thus advertising seeks to ensure sales, while production schedules are geared to meet projected demand. These plans can be implemented because firms are able to control their prices by insulating themselves from some of the effects of their rivals' competition. Most contemporary innovations by firms occur as a result of their successful persuasion of consumers to demand particular new goods and services. Such advertising is subversive of free markets.

The increased size of the public sector within mixed economies makes a growing number of firms more dependent upon government orders to maintain their sales and profitability, while the state often directly finances their research and development programmes. The private firm as a large bureaucratic organisation becomes hardly distinguishable from public corporations. Both depend on their technostructure, the resulting 'divorce of ownership from control' creating the potentiality to pursue objectives other than profit. Within the private sector, profit maximisation normally still predominates; the specialists who serve a particular corporation depend upon it for incomes and careers, and generally develop a sense of loyalty towards it. They possess a powerful motive to promote its profitability, but the complexity of multidimensional choice in conditions of uncertainty implies that maximising profits, even in the limited sense of preferring more to less profitable options, is not a simple matter. The precise consequences are controversial, but the traditional antithesis drawn between public and private enterprise is increasingly irrelevant as large private companies reap the benefits of economies of scale, currently on a multinational basis.

As citizens become increasingly interdependent, greater government control of economic activity is required; Heilbroner (1960) argues that the political sphere of capitalist democracy gradually usurps its economic sphere. The specific motivation behind such policies is to preserve rather than to undo capitalism, but Heilbroner believes that in practice their ultimate effect is to undermine. In this context Galbraith points to the difficulties governments often face in raising the revenue to finance their activities, as few vested interests achieve any direct gain from taxation while there is a lack of advertising in support of state expenditure. Consequently the provision of goods and services is biased towards those produced in the private sector, but the resulting combination of 'private affluence and public squalor' generates disruptive social tensions.

Galbraith seeks to replace Marshall's 'representative firm' by a concept of 'the new industrial state'. His account of the behaviour of giant firms appears plausible, or at least worth analysis, but it has obtained few successes as an ideological doctrine. As he observes, a large proportion of the professional class in modern capitalism is directly or indirectly employed by large corporations which the educational system largely serves. Therefore those occupying positions of power normally are able to prevent radical views from penetrating orthodoxy.

NOTES

1 Schumpeter wrote that the large corporation 'not only ousts the smaller or medium-sized firm and expropriates its owners, but in the end it also ousts the entrepreneur and expropriates the bourgeoisie as a class, which in the process stands to lose not only its income but also what is infinitely more important, its function'.

2 Burkitt (1979) discussed the pivotal significance of periodic unemployment for the operation of labour markets.
3 Burkitt (1982) developed this argument.
4 Chapters Five and Seven discuss the phenomenon of alienation in greater detail.
5 Described by Schumpeter as 'the naughty child that tells unpleasant truths'.

10 The Modern Revival of Radical Political Economy

The last twenty years witnessed increased dissatisfaction with the methodology of orthodox economics.[1] This dissatisfaction is illustrated by renewed interest in Marxism, by the radical arguments developed during the Capital Controversy and by the formation of the Union of Radical Political Economists in the United States and the Conference of Socialist Economists in Britain. Radicals believe that the inadequacy of economic analysis for explaining contemporary issues is due to the fundamental assumptions that lie at its heart and provide the criteria by which an 'economic problem' is defined. The deficiencies of the neoclassical paradigm documented in Chapter Eight originated this belief, but it sharpened during the Capital Controversy of the 1960s, which established the existence of logical ambiguities at the heart of neoclassical theory. Such ambiguities stimulated attempts to construct a radical alternative. These developments are the subject of this chapter.

THE CAPITAL CONTROVERSY

The Capital Controversy arose from analysis of changes in the distribution of a growing national income. Behind the theoretical discussion lies a fundamental divergence of views concerning the validity of the marginalist approach; neoclassicals[2] regard distribution as one facet of the theory of value, while radicals consider that it should be analysed in different terms preceding the theory of value in priority though not in time. Ideological differences are intimately linked to this debate, neoclassicals neglecting the sociological characteristics of capitalism which radicals see as central determinants of distribution. Dissatisfaction with the marginal productivity theory stimulates attempts to develop models in which pricing is an outcome of distribution rather than the reverse.

For neoclassicals the rate of profit measures the marginal productivity of capital, *i.e.* profits derive from capital's contribution to output. Capital is defined as profit-earning finance embodied in a stock of resources, which is a factor of production of equivalent analytical status to labour. Individuals enjoy the ownership of certain endowments, which they employ to maximise self-interest by engaging in market exchange. They voluntarily make contracts and receive a payment determined by the productivity of their services. Varying urgencies of need, the possibility of class struggle and the existence of differential power are ignored as attention is focussed upon the equilibrium set of factor prices which optimises resource allocation by maximising utility,[3] because each factor is employed to the point where its marginal product[4] equals its price. The prices of individual factors are aggregated to obtain macrodistribution, so that neoclassicals locate the determination of income shares within the general pricing of commodities[5]; although factors are exchanged in their own specific markets, their prices are ultimately determined by the product market from which sociological data are excluded as exogenously formed constraints.

The cornerstone of this paradigm is that the marginal productivity of a factor governs its pricing, but such a use of marginal productivity requires two essential conditions:

(i) It must be possible to vary the quantity of one factor used during production while the quantity of at least one other is fixed. This condition can be met only if factors are homogenous or reducible to some homogenous quantity.

(ii) It must be possible to construct a production function, *i.e.* a schedule representing all the factor combinations possible at a given state of technical knowledge, each point indicating a distinct technique for producing a particular commodity; in competitive equilibrium the rate of factor substitution (or its inverse, the ratio of marginal productivities) equals the ratio of factor prices. When the latter changes, the minimum cost technique alters in such a way that, if wages rise relative to profits, capital intensive techniques become increasingly profitable.

Therefore in neoclassical general equilibrium theory the distribution of income is determined by the initial distribution of resources, consumer preferences, firms' production functions, and the behavioural assumptions made, such as profit and utility maximisation. Radicals question the foundation of this theory. They argue that its exogenous data are more significant than its endogenous variables; since the structure of property ownership results from the division between wages and profit, it becomes the central feature around which to develop models of distribution. However, the Capital Controversy inaugurated a novel state in the debate because it raised doubts about the logical tenability of neoclassical theory even within its own assumptions.[6]

Under capitalism the resource conventionally termed 'capital' possesses at least three dimensions:

(i) the stock of equipment and materials which enables workers to generate marketable commodities,

(ii) the command over finance which permits employers to organise the production of goods which they can sell at a profit,

(iii) (i) and (ii) comprise the physical aspects of capital, but it also embodies a social property relationship, *i.e.* capitalists own the means of production and workers must sell labour power to them to obtain a livelihood. In an alternative type of economic organisation, these ownership relations may disappear as physical and financial resources only become social capital (dimension (iii)) if owned by non-labourers. Private appropriation of the product derived from the intangible assets of the whole community requires a class monopoly of ownership of the means of production.

The Capital Controversy initially centred on the search for a unit to measure aggregate capital, independent of distribution and relative prices, so that it can be used without circular reasoning to explain income shares. Sraffa (1960) demonstrated the lack of any coherent logical basis behind attempts to discover such a unit of measurement. He showed that the relative prices of two commodities change when the wage rate and the rate of profit alter. Consequently the value of capital goods depends upon distribution, a phenomenon that cannot be 'reconciled with *any* notion of capital as a measurable quantity independent of distribution and prices'. Therefore the orthodox contention that the marginal product of capital determines the rate of profit becomes meaningless. The rate of profit must be known before capital can be aggregated into a single quantity to determine its marginal product (*i.e.* the effect on output of varying capital by a single unit); the value of the capital stock depends upon its prevailing rate of return and cannot be used to explain it. Consequently income determination must be determined exogenously from marginal products.

Blaug (1974) is incorrect when arguing that 'the problem of measuring labour is on all fours with the problem of measuring capital'. Capital goods can only be aggregated in terms of their equilibrium prices in which a rate of profit is contained, but aggregate labour in terms of person hours can be obtained by supposing relative wages are constant and using them as weights. Moreover, a measure of the workforce is less significant since, while there must be a uniform rate of profit at long period competitive equilibrium even if capital is heterogenous, there need not be a uniform wage rate unless labour is homogenous. Therefore the rate of profit may be taken as exogenous when calculating the capital stock of one firm, but this procedure involves circular reasoning when constructing a measure of aggregate capital.

Bhaduri (1969) proved that the marginal productivity of capital does not in general equal the rate of profit. Let:

- Y = net national income measured in a homogenous consumption good;
- K = value of capital, net of depreciation, in terms of the same consumption good;
- L = number of employed workers;
- r = the rate of profit, a pure number per unit of time;
- w = the real wage rate per worker per unit of time in terms of the consumption good.

Assuming that net national income is distributed between profits and wages,

(1) $Y = Kr + Lw$

Without any loss of generality, equation (1) can be normalised by setting $L = 1$ and writing in per worker measure,

(2) $Y = kr + w$

Since equation (2) is purely definitional, it holds for all economies where net income is distributed between profits and wages, and should be compatible with any acceptable treatment of capital including that of marginal productivity theory. This is not, however, generally true, as a comparison of two hypothetical economies indicates, each marginally different in terms of output per head (y), value of capital per head (k) and their respective wage-profit configurations (w and r). The comparison is achieved by totally differentiating (2), yielding,

$$(3)\ dy = r\,dk + k\,dr + dw$$

It is clear from definitional equation (3) that the marginal product of capital, *i.e.* $\frac{dy}{dk}$ does not *in general* equal the rate of profit (r). They become equal only in the *special* case where by chance or by assumption,[7]

$$(4)\ k\,dr + dw = 0, \text{ which in turn implies that}$$

$$(5)\ -\frac{dw}{dr} = k$$

The productivity of physical capital goods (created by a past labour process) can be distinguished from the ability of capitalists to secure a proportion of the product as profits merely through their ownership of property.

RESWITCHING AND CAPITAL REVERSING

Recognition that reswitching and capital reversing might possibly occur was a by-product of the Capital Controversy. *Reswitching* exists when the same technique is the most profitable at two or more separated values of the rate of profit, even though other techniques are most profitable at intermediate rates of profit. *Capital Reversing* refers to a positive rela;tionship between the value of capital and the rate of profit when switching from one technique to another. The theoretical validity of each possibility is now generally regarded as unassailable.

Reswitching and capital reversing arise once there are heterogenous capital goods and non-uniform inputs of labour into production at different points in time. It is the differential impact of given changes in labour inputs over time, and the consequent variation in the discounting factor, that is responsible for these phenomena. To neoclassicals, they destroy the wider application of certain simple parables but do not impugn the general validity of their methodology; to radicals, they constitute a death blow to neoclassicism by destroying the concept of a demand curve for capital in the sense of a unique, inverse relationship between rates of profit and values of capital. They cannot be relegated to the category of specialised difficulties because they raise the general problem of the relativity of price determination to income distribution.

The mechanics of reswitching depend upon the time pattern

of productive processes. The cost of a commodity is reached through the summation of a vertical series of stages of production, each consisting of a labour input plus a commodity input produced during an earlier period. Consider two commodities, one with larger labour inputs bunched at recent dates and the other with much smaller labour inputs bunched at distant dates. With low wages and high interest the first may be cheaper despite its greater wage bill. As wages rise and interest falls, the second at some stage becomes cheapest because of its lesser wage costs. An orthodox production function can be fitted in this case.

Suppose one commodity has most of its labour inputs applied at an intermediate date, while another has some labour at a recent time. It is possible for the second commodity to possess the cost advantage at medium ranges of interest and wages, but for the first to be cheaper *both* at very high rates of interest with equivalently low wages *and* at very low rates of interest with high wages. The reason is the possibility of differences in the compounding effect of interest rate changes on the comparative cost of inputs of distant and intermediate dates. Relative prices, therefore, are determined by the varying proportions of labour and other inputs at successive layers of production, and the relative prices of two commodities may move with a wage reduction in an opposite direction to what is expected on the basis of their labour intensities of production.

Moreover, input prices may move so as to reverse the ordering of two commodities in terms of labour-capital ratios (capital reversing). The backward switch to greater capital intensity with lower wages is determined by the time pattern of the relevant techniques. If the relative value of the capital goods required by any two productive systems remains constant as the rate of profit changes, a fall in the rate of profit inevitably cheapens the more capital intensive of the two. However, a fall in the rate of profit could reduce the relative value of the capital goods used in the less capital intensive system and make it cheaper than the more capital intensive alternative. If that occurs, substitution by consumers lowers the ratio of capital to labour over the economy as profits decline.

Therefore, if the rate of profit changes it affects the cost of different techniques in varying proportions. If a less mechanised technique takes longer to construct, and possesses a different

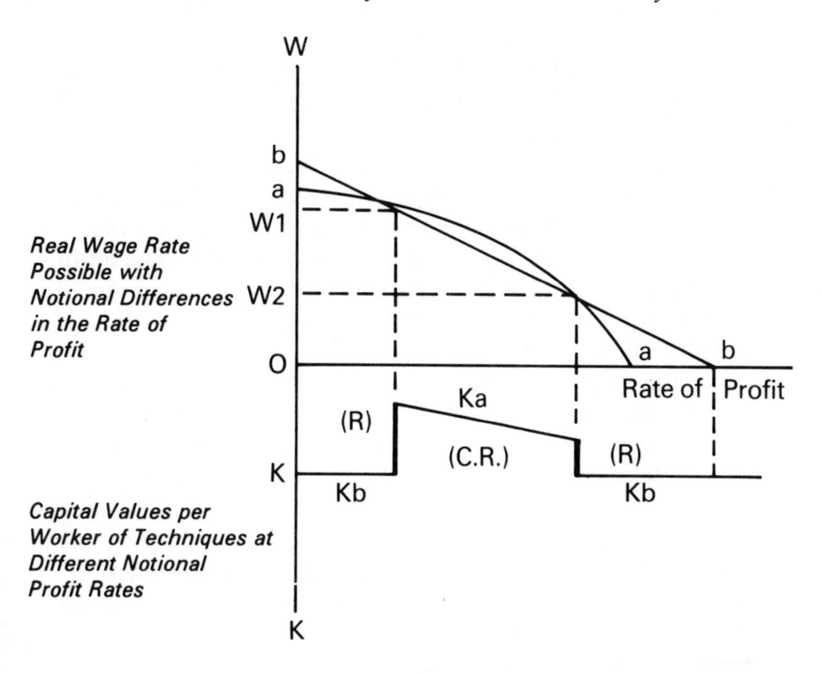

Figure One

time pattern of inputs, its production costs may be affected relatively more due to the different amount of labour applied at different dates, so that at a lower rate of profit highly mechanised techniques become less profitable. When the effect of profitability changes on capital costs is considered, the conventional association between the capital intensity of production and the rate of profit may not hold.

Figure One links reswitching to capital reversing. Each point on the curves in the upper portion shows for a single technique the rate of profit associated with a given wage rate. The lower portion illustrates the value of capital per worker at different rates of profit. Two techniques are possible, a and b,[8] with Ka and Kb representing the value of capital per head under each at different profit rates. At real wages above W1 the most profitable technique is b, between W1 and W2 it is a, while below W2 it becomes b again. The vertical shifts in the bottom line represent reswitching, while its downward slope indicates capital reversing.

THE IMPLICATIONS OF THE CAPITAL CONTROVERSY AND THE RESWITCHING DEBATE

The heterogenity of capital equipment and the varying time pattern of productive inputs give rise to reswitching and capital reversing, which make it impossible to say unambiguously that:

(i) a fall in the rate of profit alters the ranking of techniques by profitability in a uni-directional manner, or

(ii) a fall in the rate of profit necessarily increases the capital intensity of production.

The notion of the demand for capital as a function of the rate of profit appears untenable, so that it is impossible to provide a determinate rate of profit in terms of capital's relative scarcity.

As Ferguson (1969) conceded, continued acceptance of the neoclassical theory of distribution requires faith that reswitching and reversing occur only rarely in practice, but even granting this assumption the other arguments ventilated in the Capital Controversy imply that the 'value of capital' is neither a useful nor a necessary concept. However, it performs two crucial functions for the political economy of capitalism:

(i) At a *practical* level, evaluation of machines of different types and ages is needed to settle transactions among capitalists, to determine the value of the legally exclusive right to use machinery and the worth of the pieces of paper embodying such rights.

(ii) It fulfills the *ideological* role of appearing to break the direct link between the time pattern of labour inputs and the time pattern of output into which any technology can be resolved. It substitutes a relationship between present labour and present output, to which the current value of the capital stock provides an indispensable contribution. It is a mythical construction whereby the past and future are telescoped into the present, but it enables attention to be diverted from past labour towards the contemporary value of its embodiment, whose productivity is seen as a justification for attributing profit to its owners.

ALTERNATIVE THEORIES OF DISTRIBUTION

Radicals believe that the Capital Controversy and the phenomena of reswitching and capital reversing destroy both the concept of an aggregate production function and the orthodox demand schedules for capital and labour. To fill the void left by these deficiencies, an alternative framework is required in which distribution is determined independently of relative prices.[9] Given *either* the rate of profit *or* the wage rate *and* the technological conditions of production, the other factor price and commodity prices can be established. Various models of macrodistribution have been developed in the last twenty-five years; most reflect, in different ways, Sraffa's belief that distribution is an outcome of social conflict rather than a technical matter where 'the necessary subsistence of the workers is not differentiated from the fuel for the engines or the feed for the cattle'. Thus radicals highlight the specific institutional structure of capitalism as crucial to distribution; competition ensures equal rates of profit across industries at long-run equilibrium and the mobility of capital which brings this about, together with the technical coefficients of production, determines relative prices. Recent radical theories attempt to close Sraffa's system by explaining the division between profits and wages. A variety of possible explanations have emerged:

(i) *Sraffa's Theory*: Sraffa (1960) undermined the neoclassical theory of distribution by proving that the rate of profit and relative prices could be determined without reference to demand. It is possible in principle, although it may be complicated practically, to establish the price of a commodity provided only that the rate of profit and the direct and indirect labour inputs into its production are known, without making any assumptions about the behaviour of individual agents. Sraffa demonstrated the existence of an inverse wage-profit relation, with competition ensuring that at any given wage the productive technique chosen is the one that generates the highest rate of profit. However, one technique may sustain the highest rate of profit for two or more different wage levels so that no unique correspondence exists between the particular technique used and any specific distribution.

Sraffa restated the conflict between capitalists and workers by formulating the relation between real wages and the rate of profit, but there is no simple way of closing his system, *i.e.* of deciding which point on the wage-profit frontier is actually reached. Real wages cannot be taken as directly fixed by class struggle because collective bargaining determines money wages, while the real wage also depends upon the behaviour of prices. Once the rate of exploitation is given, the entire structure of relative prices is determined under competitive equilibrium, although the explanation of exploitation is controversial. Sraffa suggested that the rate of profit, although an object of social conflict, may be related to money rates of interest. Robinson (1961) argued that this suggestion cannot furnish a comprehensive explanation, because the rate of interest, the reward of waiting on rentier wealth, is determined in money markets and is usually lower and subject to less risk than investments in productive resources. Consequently radicals need to look elsewhere to close the Sraffian system.

(ii) *Post-Keynesian Theory*: Certain post-Keynesians, notably Kaldor (1956) and Pasinetti (1962), have suggested that the rate of profit is determined by the differential saving propensities associated with different classes of income receivers and by the rate of growth given *either* by the expansion of the labour force and neutral technical progress *or* by capitalists' investment decisions. They extend Keynes' (1936) analysis into the long run to explain the rate of profit by the speed of accumulation and the excess of consumption out of profits over saving out of wages.

Kaldor (1956) assumed a state of full employment, so that national income (Y) is given and divided between two classes, labour (W) and capital (P). The marginal propensity to save is smaller from W than P, because on average workers receive smaller incomes while a high proportion of profit is retained within companies without being immediately consumed. Kaldor made two further assumptions; that the marginal propensities to save for both capitalists and workers are constant over time and that investment is the independent causal variable to which savings accommodate through movements in distributive shares. Within this framework Kaldor uses the Keynesian multiplier to explain, not the level of employment, but the distribution of a given output.

(6) $Y = W + P$

(7) $I = S$

(8) $S = Sw + Sp$

Taking investment as given and assuming proportional saving functions, $Sw = swW$ and $Sp = spP$, then:

(9) $I = spP + swW = spP + sw(Y - P) = (sp - sw)P + swY$

(10) $\frac{I}{Y} = (sp - sw)\frac{P}{Y} + sw$

(11) $\frac{P}{Y} = \frac{1}{(Sp - Sw)} \times \frac{I}{Y} - \frac{Sw}{Sp - Sw}$

Therefore, given a constant propensity to save for capitalists and workers, the share of profits in national income depends on the ratio of investment to output.

These equations are formally valid, but their interpretative significance rests on the plausibility of Kaldor's assumptions. The maintenance of full employment implies that P's behaviour relative to W depends upon demand movements. A rise in investment, and therefore of aggregate demand, leads to increases in prices and profit margins as output is at its maximum. Conversely declining investment and demand produces a fall in prices, and thus of profits, relative to the money wage level. Therefore disparities between planned investment and planned savings generate distributive changes that restore their equality due to the different class propensities to save, the level of saving altering with income shifts between capitalists and workers. Equilibrium will be attained so long as the propensity to save from profits is the greater, a condition which is likely to be fulfilled empirically.

If workers' net savings are zero, profits equal the sum of investment plus capitalist consumption, *i.e.*

(12) $P = \frac{1}{Sp} I$

Equation (12) summarises the position in which 'capitalists earn what they spend and workers spend what they earn'. Workers' income is the residual left over from corporate decisions concerning investment and capitalist consumption; the more capitalists consume, the scarcer capital becomes and the higher profits rise. If workers' savings are positive, profits are correspondingly reduced.

Figure Two illustrates Kaldor's model. $\frac{I}{Y}$ is autonomously determined, while $\frac{S}{Y}$ is a function of $\frac{P}{Y}$ because of the lower

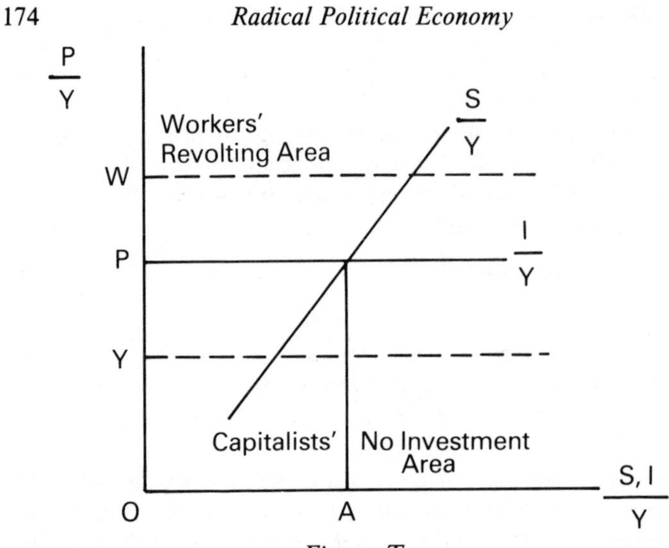

Figure Two

marginal propensity to save out of wages. If SW = O, $\frac{S}{Y}$ starts at the origin; if Sp = 1, it is a 45° line. Were $\frac{P}{Y}$ not initially at the value where $\frac{S}{Y}$ and $\frac{I}{Y}$ intersect, planned saving would stand in such a relationship to planned investment that, via the impact of excess demand or excess supply on prices, income distribution changes until $\frac{S}{Y} = \frac{I}{Y}$. If $\frac{I}{Y}$ is OA, $\frac{P}{Y}$ is OP. Any increase in $\frac{I}{Y}$ leads to a higher equilibrium value of $\frac{P}{Y}$ and thus to a decline in the share of income going to labour. Workers gain from rises in their propensity to save, while capitalists gain from spending by themselves or workers.

Kaldor imposed two limits on the operation of his model, beyond which it cannot function:

(i) the real wage cannot fall below the level of subsistence (OW in Figure Two) for otherwise the supply of labour shrinks, and

(ii) the profit share must be sufficient to induce capitalists to invest, *i.e.* profits cannot shrink permanently below their 'normal' level (OY in Figure Two).

A number of attempts have been made to test Kaldor's hypothesis empirically. Given stable savings propensities, it predicts that a rise in the proportion of income that is invested leads to a fall in labour's relative share. Reder (1959) and Gallaway (1964) found the evidence consistent with this prediction for the United States. Gallaway discovered that $\frac{I}{Y}$

changes correctly forecast wage share movements in twenty-three of thirty-one years between 1929 and 1960, although the war period (1942 to 1946) did not exhibit this tendency.

Assessments of Kaldor's contribution[10] must at this stage rest on theoretical arguments, particularly about the strength of its assumptions. One focal point for consideration is the assumption of full employment. If total income is not given, equality of investment and savings may be achieved through income movements rather than by distributive changes. However, higher investment may lead to both an increase in income and a rise in capital's relative share. These two outcomes need not be mutually exclusive, which complicates but does not invalidate Kaldor's hypothesis.

A more serious issue is whether Kaldor's equations represent the causes or the effects of the profit share attaining a certain level. Bronfenbrenner (1971) argued that it is more plausible to see them as effects; with full employment determined exogenously, a higher profit share generates faster growth and/or a greater capital-output ratio. He saw no reason to suppose that causation flows the other way. In a sense Kaldor's theory is tautological, but its analytical content arises from interpreting the association between the ratio of investment to income and the profit share. Kaldor argued that investment is the independent variable, while Bronfenbrenner believed that the reverse causal sequence operates. Kaldor's view implies that:

(i) entrepreneurs cannot substitute between factors of production, *i.e.* production coefficients are fixed,

(ii) wage changes do not affect decisions to invest,

(iii) innovations are independent of factor prices, so that high wages do not stimulate labour-saving inventions nor low wages generate labour-using devices.

Subjective opinions on the validity of these implications vary and determine judgements on the significance of Kaldor's theory. Given its assumptions his model holds so that it stands or falls with their acceptibility. Even if they are accepted, additional hypotheses are required to explain the formation of the minimum wage acceptable to workers and the rate of profit regarded as normal by capitalists. These constraining standards become particularly significant in historical situations where they conflict or reduce the distributive shifts analysed by Kaldor to a narrow range.[11]

(iii) *Neo-Marxist Theory:* Many radicals, *e.g.* Robinson (1965), Nell (1967) and Bhaduri (1969), redefine Marx's theory of exploitation in terms of relative bargaining strength between capitalists and workers. Competition ensures the equality of profit rates in all industries which, together with the production coefficients, determine the price structure. Capitalists compete for profit outlets but they collude, tacitly or openly, against workers during collective bargaining. Wages are negotiated in money terms but their precise level is influenced by the power and past experience of the groups on each side of the market. Collective bargaining reflecting the state of class conflict, market forces exhibited in choices of technique and Keynesian influences of aggregate demand and the equality of investment and saving interact with technical progress and population growth to determine simultaneously the level of activity and income distribution.

Recent neo-Marxist theory emphasises the 'perennial gale' of capitalist-worker antagonism based on a rigorous mathematical proof of the inverse relationship between profits and wages. The latter is not invalidated by the fact that both may increase with technological change, since before and after the impact of innovation distributive shares are fixed, at least in money terms, by the class struggle. These models establish that capital is both a quantity and a social relation, but fail to prove why the rates of profit and exploitation remain positive at long-run competitive equilibrium.

Bose (1975) attempted to fill this gap by developing a 'post-Marxian' theory of why the rate of capitalist exploitation is positive in a commodity production model. His theory, which stresses the coercive power of capitalists over workers, is based on the following propositions:

(i) The basic motivation of capitalist production is accumulation for expanded reproduction.

(ii) From (i), capitalism would never come into existence if profit was non-positive and would come to an end if it permanently fell to zero, although it could also end when profits were positive if 'conditions ripen' to render accumulation on the basis of private enterprise obsolete.

(iii) From (i) and (ii), the following equilibrium conditions hold; the share of land rents must leave the maximum rate of profit (corresponding to a hypothetical zero wage) positive, while the share of wages from this maximum potential profit must allow a positive actual rate of profit.

(iv) However, (a) a secular rise in workers' living standards, and/or, (b) scarcity of land due to expanded reproduction, tends to increase real wages and rent, so pressing against available profit margins.

(v) But the pressure to accumulate stimulates capitalists to introduce technical improvements, which are land-saving or increase labour's productivity. These maintain a positive rate of profit, so sustaining the basis for continued accumulation.

(iv) *Institutionalist Theory:* A number of sociological theories follow Mill's (1848) summary of distribution as 'a matter of human institution solely'. These have been developed extensively in France where the leading exponent is Marchal (1957), who derived inspiration from the institutional changes of the last century. Several factors contributed to convert distribution from a micro-economic event into a nationwide bargaining affair. Technical change produced larger firms, which generated greater labour solidarity and closer employer relationships. Increased mobility and closer contacts widened the scope for coordinated action. Moreover, incomes are no longer regarded purely as a price but as a payment signifying status, while their function in maintaining purchasing power is taken into account.

These influences create a national bargaining process in which several groups are distinguished by type of income and by their behaviour in the distributive struggle. A macrodistribution theory should study the interdependent division of total income between these groups. Marchal does not stop therefore at a division between capitalists and workers, nor does he restrict analysis to the trinity of rent, profits and wages. He introduces as many income categories as the bargaining mechanism of a particular period 'requires', for example he draws a distinction between industrial and agricultural profits.

Any study of distribution must analyse the behaviour of these more or less homogenous groups, which endeavour to defend their absolute and relative living standards by both economic and political activity. Consequently market structures and institutional data cannot be taken as given (unlike the era of purely individualistic action), but are variables which can be altered during group struggles over income shares. Past real income is a crucial rallying point for collective action. When it is threatened, social equilibrium is lost and tensions arise. These generate a variety of economic and social processes, *e.g.* inflation, changes in output and migration between groups. Gradually adjustment occurs either because a group reconquers its former standard or because the notion of what constitutes a 'proper' income is revised after some group members leave and the rest accept deterioration.

Institutionalist theory does not necessarily conflict with post-Keynesian and neo-Marxist models, since the propensities and ratios used in the latter could be translated into the determinants of group action. Traditional economic categories require supplementation by sociological influences, although the French have yet to give their theories sufficient formal strength. Radicals, whichever alternative hypothesis they prefer, see 'the factor of production, capital' as an abstraction without any specific historical counterpart. To use it for a theory of distribution under capitalism, its ownership dimension which gives rise to profits must be considered explicitly.

THE POLICY IMPLICATIONS OF RECENT RADICAL ANALYSIS

The Capital Controversy, the discovery of reswitching and capital reversing, and the development of alternative distribution theories carry implications for those seeking to achieve a transition to socialism. They suggest that a necessary, although far from sufficient, condition is the wresting of control over accumulation from capitalists, whose hegemony depends upon their day-to-day dominance of business decision-making. Therefore policies and institutional structures which enable labour to determine capital accumulation[12] need to be devised. Simultaneously an increase in total investment will augment social welfare. The marginal productivity of an investment to society is reflected by the additional profits and the growth in the wage bill that it generates. However, capitalists classify only the former as a benefit when taking decisions, and this tends to create an under-investment problem. Consequently, accelerated capital accumulation and its control by workers are two central radical objectives emphasised by recent economic debates.

A crucial equation derived from post-Keynesian distribution theory is:

(13) Profit = Investment + Capitalist Consumption – Workers' Saving.

Workers' savings reduce total profits and increase their relative income share, but the ratio of investment to output determines distribution at given savings' propensities. Thus egalitarian policies can take three forms (or combinations of them); to lower investment, to reduce capitalist consumption or to raise workers' savings. The scope for effective action in each of these spheres is limited within contemporary mixed economies.

The first possibility, a reduction in investment, is contradictory. Such a reduction increases labour's share of national income, but less investment implies diminished productive efficiency and thus a smaller future real income.

The second alternative, a fall in capitalist consumption, appears more promising, but property incomes in a capitalist economy also provide the source for accumulation. The ability of redistributive measures to increase labour's share depends upon the extent to which they reduce capitalist consumption without endangering the growth of the capital stock. If capitalists' marginal propensity to consume is large, considerable inroads into their consumption are possible, but if it is small such a feat is unlikely. The probability is that the marginal propensity to consume from property incomes is low, partly becasue these are received by the richest individuals and partly because most profit accrues to companies, which allocate a high proportion to reserves. Consumption patterns are frequently rigid because a degree of luxury based on past experience is widely regarded as essential, with savings being depleted to resist any reduction. A fall in capitalist incomes tends to be reflected in accumulation, so that the scope for labour to make permanent gains is limited.

The third option, raising workers' savings, provides the most accessible route to redistribution. However, as the level of saving is mainly determined by income, workers possess little oppportunity to increase the proportion of total savings which they supply. A number of schemes have been advocated to stimulate workers' saving, for example Eltis (1973) suggested a wealth tax coupled with subsidies for savings schemes patronised by small and middle income recipients, but progress will be slow on past evidence.

The limitations of each strategy imply that a fairly rigid lower limit to the profit share exists under contemporary socio-economic conditions. It places severe constraints upon re-distributive policies, which can be removed only by institutional reforms that break the link between profits and personal income, so enabling investment to rise without increasing inequality.

EMPLOYEE INVESTMENT FUNDS: A MECHANISM FOR SOCIALIST TRANSITION?

Proposals for employee investment funds developed in the 1970s in Scandanavia as a method of accelerating capital accumulation, while simultaneously establishing a trend towards greater equality through a growth in the proportion of capital owned by workers. Employee investment funds re-distribute by transferring part of profits to trade union control rather than by socialising the capital stock directly. Although initiating a fundamental change in future economic organisation, they utilise a gradualist strategy that may render them politically feasible in a non-revolutionary situation.

Burkitt (1983) attempted to construct a comprehensive programme, within this framework, consisting of four essential components:

(i) *Private sector employee investment funds* — based on the Swedish proposals whereby companies with more than a hundred employees[13] transfer a portion of their total profit (currently suggested at twenty per cent) in the form of newly issued shares to employee investment funds administered by the relevant trade unions. This transferred profit remains within the firm for reinvestment. The voting rights of the stock belong to the unions, which elect directors in proportion to the relative size of their equity stake for a four-year period, half retiring or standing for re-election every two years. On present rates of growth, the most profitable Swedish firms would become worker-controlled in approximately thirty years, while trade unions are more immediately able to supervise, and where necessary, check management. After fifty to sixty years the majority of equity capital would be collectively owned. Under such a scheme, the accountability of employee investment funds to their members becomes crucial. The danger of an elite emerging is minimised by periodic re-election, while the apex of the power pyramid is at least wider than currently.

(ii) *Public sector wage and salary funds*—in an economy based upon labour management, certain public goods provided by the state remain essential. The existence of a public sector necessitates a variation on employee investment funds, since profits either do not exist or are subject to government determination. Danish proposals could be developed whereby the state pays contributions, based on the size of the wage and salary bill, which are invested in enterprises chosen by unions. These gradually become subject to the control of their own workforce with public employees in the role of minority external shareholders.

(iii) *Economy-wide labour development funds*—financed in each sector by a tax on the wage and salary bill and controlled by the relevant unions, to be used as sources for new investment in industries other than those in which their members are employed. Unions are legally compelled to apply these deposits to industrial development in labour-managed firms. They do not buy shares on the stock market, but participate directly in existing and new enterprises on the basis of their financial holdings. Economy-wide funds provide workers with interests and influence beyond their own firm and prevent industrial democracy from degenerating into sectional 'workers' capitalism'.

(iv) *Central government functions*—in recent years theoretical models of economies operating under labour management have been constructed. These conclude that such a system, under the same technical and market conditions as a capitalist economy, is equally capable of achieving optimum resource allocation. Advocates of self-management, *e.g.* Vanek (1970), claim that this conclusion supports their case. However, the discussion in Chapter Seven established the need for a co-ordinating state administration to resolve potential conflicts by defining the conditions under which employee investment funds operate. For instance, accumulation of foreign exchange reserves is a crucial objective for countries attempting substantial redistribution, to permit automony from foreign pressure, protect against unfavourable international developments and safeguard against net outflows of capital. As employee investment funds grow, labour dominates industrial decision-making, yet the community as a whole must, through the government, reserve the ultimate authority to overrule labour-managed enterprises. Employee investment funds achieve optimal efficiency only within an overall structure of democratic planning through state institutions.

The principal advantages of employee investment funds are their role in reducing inequality of wealth ownership and their long period effect on investment. They gradually become a dominant force in capital accumulation, converting it into a socially managed trust. However, it is essential that any long-run strategy of redistribution yields immediate benefits for workers; employee investment funds do so through increased authority in the workplace,[14] in addition to the jobs and incomes created by the additional accumulation diverted from capitalist consumption. They could initiate economic development, while simultaneously proving a more effective redistributor than fiscal measures and providing industrial democracy without bureaucratic management. A comprehensive scheme of the type outlined above is a vehicle for increasing both efficiency and equality.

CONCLUSION

In recent years the focus of debate between orthodox and radical economists has shifted from specifying the appropriate range and assumptions of economic models to the logical consistency of the neoclassical paradigm. The phenomenon of reswitching and capital reversing make neoclassical distribution theory harder to apply, while the Capital Controversy demonstrated that the fundamental concept of the marginal productivity of aggregate capital was meaningless. The rate of profit must be known before the total capital stock can be measured, so that use of the latter's marginal product to determine equilibrium profits involves circular reasoning. Sraffa (1960) showed that once the rate of profit or the real wage and the production coefficients are known, the other factor prices and the price structure of commodities can be established. A number of radical distribution theories have been constructed in the last twenty-five years; none has yet gained complete acceptance among economists, but these theories share a common core in emphasising the centrality of the accumulation process and the need for its control by labour if transition to socialism is to be achieved. Much work, at both a theoretical level and in designing policy proposals, remains to be performed, but this area is likely to expand and prove an exciting field of development in the years ahead.

NOTES

1. In this book orthodox economics is defined as the body of ideas synthesised by Samuelson (1955) in his reconciliation of neoclassical theories of value and distribution with Keynesian doctrines of macro-equilibrium. Conventional economists have refined and extended Samuelson's synthesis, but the pattern of their thought remains within the framework he established. Brittan (1973) provided a more recent summary of the essentials of 'liberal market orthodoxy'.
2. Defined as those who in general draw upon Samuelson's synthesis discussed in Note One.
3. In terms of Pareto optimality as defined in Chapter Eight.
4. Defined under perfect competition as a factor's marginal physical product multiplied by the price of the commodity it produces; in imperfectly competitive markets as marginal physical product multiplied by marginal revenue.
5. Johnson (1973) wrote: 'the major contribution of marginal productivity theory was to point out that the theory of factor prices and the distribution of income is only one aspect of the general theory of pricing and one aspect of general equilibrium theory'.
6. Political ideology is at the root of this dispute; if tastes, technology and factor supplies determine relative shares, class struggle becomes pointless because each individual is paid according to his or her contribution to production.
7. Samuelson (1962) secured such results by assuming that a uniform capital-labour ratio existed in all branches of production. In this situation prices are proportional to labour inputs at every rate of profit, but whenever technical relations vary, no single relation exists between a specific capital-labour ratio and a certain wage or profit rate.
8. Technique b is a straight line in the upper portion, *i.e.* it involves a uniform capital-labour ratio in the production of both capital and consumer goods, so that the line representing the value of capital per worker (Kb) retains the same slope despite differences in the rate of profit.
9. Blaug (1974) argued from a neoclassical standpoint that 'the great mystery of the modern theory of distribution is, actually, why anyone regards the share of wages and profits in total income as an interesting problem'. He believed that relative shares are the outcome of such a wide

variety of forces that any theory attempting to deal with them has to make so many simplifying assumptions that its results are simply intellectual curios. He concluded that no persuasive reason exists to justify pre-occupation with distributive shares.

10 Pasinetti (1962) extended Kaldor's model by showing that the rate of return on capital during a process of steady-state growth depends directly on the rate of growth of the labour force and inversely on the savings propensity of profit receivers, some of whom are likely to be workers earning profits on invested savings. This discovery has become known as Pasinetti's Paradox, whereby the rate of profit is independent of the propensity to save out of wages.

11 Burkitt (1979) explored this issue in detail.

12 Currently capitalists control the accumulation of capital both by taking investment decisions and by organising their own and others' saving.

13 The figures proposed by the Swedish Social Democrats can be varied to conform to different national situations. In Sweden the Social Democrats are finalising legislation following their election success in 1982.

14 Workers' control could be brought about directly through legislation or industrial action, but employee investment funds enable labour to acquire increasing influence through the shareholding which they acquire.

11 Conclusion

Radicals possess two defining qualities; a commitment to the deprived based upon a recognition of their dignity and rights, and a belief that much of human suffering is avoidable. Economics lies at the heart of radical thought, because most misery in the contemporary world is basedupon material want. Radical political economy offers a global view of how societies function in the economic and related spheres of human action, which, to be successful, must be consistent with known facts, be persuasive and provide an agenda for action. Radical economics was a rapidly developing social science before 1914, possessing an underlying core of common beliefs, based chiefly on Marx, which were being extended. Subsequently it lay dormant, apart from certain isolated if sometimes influential voices,[1] until the last twenty years when it re-emerged, both to develop its own models and to criticise received theory at a methodological and substantive level. The main task of radical scholarship is to facilitate the transformation of contemporary exploitative society.

In 1983 radical political fortunes stood at a low ebb in the face of world recession and an advancing monetarist ideology, yet confidence in an ultimate socialist victory can be based on:

(i) the existence of a number of socialist countries which possess the ability to defend themselves against capitalist depredations without destroying the essence of their socialism,

(ii) the size and power of worldwide socialist movements which produce a growing radical base, and

(iii) the recent upsurge in radical economic thought which has created an intellectual platform from which further advances in understanding can be built to forge a powerful instrument of economic analysis.

A socialist world is not inevitable; it may never appear, while if it does it will only be after prolonged, intensive struggle. Yet on a radical analysis it *can* and *should* occur.

Radical political economy rests on an appraisal of a fundamental social institution—class relations and their implications. It therefore avoids the obfuscation inherent in other economic philosophies which seek to avoid this phenomenon. Its major objective is to assist in bringing about a qualitative transformation of an exploitative society, a goal requiring different focus and techniques from orthodox economics. One of its central roles is to reinterpret the massive body of present research from a specifically radical orientation. By contrast, the neoclassical orthodoxy adhered to by a majority of western economists assumes that individuals are the crucial building blocks of analysis and that the relations of production are privatised. These assumptions dominate price theory, and the efficiency properties of neoclassical solutions to economic problems are invariably based on price theory. Thus when analysing the behaviour of consumers it is assumed that the satisfaction derived by a household from its consumption is independent of the situation of other households. Socialism therefore immediately loses relevance! The corresponding assumption with regard to production units causes neoclassical helplessness in the face of monopoly, environmental pollution and ecological problems. Contemporary orthodox 'economics' based on restrictive and arbitrary assumptions needs to be reconverted into a more comprehensive 'political economy'.

The capitalist wage relation is rooted in the fact that wage and salary earners do not own the means of production. If they owned them, they would still need to work but profits would no longer accrue to a minority class possessing capital. Any programme that falls short of abolishing this wage relation has no claim to being described as socialism, although it may be a transitional stage on the way thereto. The term 'socialism' was originally coined for the purpose of designating a society in which producers own the tools with which they work. Under modern industrial conditions this cannot be achieved individually, so that the only reasonable definition of socialism centres on communal ownership. If a socialist society is defined as one in which the wage relation has been abolished, the producers placed in control of machinery and the cleavage between mental and physical labour overcome through an all-round development of human personality, the objective is still far from attainment. Workers' control of industry, achieved either by conventional nationalisation or employee investment funds, appears to be a promising strategy for economic and social transformation.

A limited optimism seems justified. Although radicals encounter difficulties operating within a relatively hostile environment, a firm base exists in terms of the economic theory outlined in previous chapters upon which to develop a substantial unity in radical orientation. This base is rooted in Marxism, but also in the recognition that Marx's analysis requires substantial revision before it can interpret twentieth-century experience. To understand Marx requires an understanding of the specific nineteenth-century context in which he developed his ideas, and his own emphasis on the centrality of the flow of history to social understanding is bound to create inadequacies in his work when discussing contemporary economies. However, he made many observations that are crucial for analysis of modern capitalism, as the discussion of Chapters Four and Five makes clear. Modern radicals derive inspiration from the fact that successful revolutions have occurred (and therefore can occur again in the future), transforming whole societies. An overriding current need is for political unity among radicals within each capitalist country; further study is a necessary condition for this to occur. Therefore the future of radical political economy is problematic, although optimistic portents can be discerned. What is certain, however, is that the issues raised by radical economists will remain central to the future of humanity and carry profound implications for the development of economics in the future.

NOTES

1 Baran (1957), Dobb (1937), Strachey (1936) and Sweezy (1946) are leading examples.

Bibliography

R. ARON (1965), *Main Currents in Sociological Thought: Volume One,* Weidenfeld and Nicolson.
K. J. ARROW (1963), *Social Choice and Individual Values*, Wiley.
A. B. ATKINSON (1972), *Unequal Shares: Wealth in Britain*, Allen Lane.
P. A. BARAN (1957), *The Political Economy of Growth*, Monthly Review Press.
P. A. BARAN and P. M. SWEEZY (1966), *Monopoly Capital*, Monthly Review Press.
I. BARRON and R. CURNOW (1979), *The Future with Microelectronics*, Frances Pinter.
C. A. and M. R. BEARD (1927), *The Rise of American Civilisation*, Macmillan.
J. D. M. BELL (1949), *Industrial Unionism: A Critical Analysis*, McNaughton and Gowenlock.
I. BERLIN (1958), *Two Concepts of Liberty*, Oxford University Press.
E. BERNSTEIN (1899), *Evolutionary Socialism*, Shocken.
A. BHADURI (1969), 'On the Significance of Recent Controversies on Capital Theory: A Marxian View', *Economic Journal.*
R. M. BLACKBURN and M. MANN (1979), *The Working Class in the Labour Market*, Macmillan.
M. BLAUG (1968), *Economic Theory in Retrospect*, Heinemann.
M. BLAUG (1974), *The Cambridge Revolution: Success or Failure? A Critical Analysis of Cambridge Theories of Value and Distribution*, Institute of Economic Affairs.
E. von BOHM-BAWERK (1896), *Karl Marx and the Close of His System*, Merlin (1975).
C. BOOTH (1904), *Life and Labour of the People in London*, Macmillan.
L. von BORTKIEWICZ (1907), 'On the Correction of Marx's Fundamental Construction in the Third Volume of "Capital"', in *Karl Marx and the Close of His System*, edited by P. M. Sweezy, Kelley (1966).
A. BOSE (1975), *Marxian and Post-Marxian Political Economy,* Penguin.
H. BRAVERMAN (1974), *Labour and Monopoly Capital*, Monthly Review Press.
J. F. BRAY (1839), *Labour's Wrongs and Labour's Remedies: or, the Age of Might and the Age of Right*, Leeds.
S. BRITTAN (1973), *Is There an Economic Consensus?* Macmillan.

M. BRONFENBRENNER (1971), *Income Distribution Theory*, Macmillan.

B. BURKITT (1979), 'Wage Restraint and the Inflation Barrier', *Review of Radical Political Economies.*

B. BURKITT (1980), *Trades Unions and Wages: Implications for Economic Theory*, Bradford University Press.

B. BURKITT (1982), 'Collective Bargaining, Inflation and Incomes Policy', *Socialist Economic Review.*

B. BURKITT (1983), 'Post-Keynesian Distribution Theory and Employee Investment Funds', *Economic Studies Quarterly.*

B. BURKITT and D. BOWERS (1979), *Trade Unions and the Economy*, Macmillan.

E. H. CHAMBERLIN (1933), *The Theory of Monopolistic Competition*, Harvard University Press.

H. A. CLEGG (1951), *Industrial Democracy and Nationalisation*, Blackwell.

G. D. H. COLE (1913), *The World of Labour*, Bell.

G. D. H. COLE (1919), *Self-Government in Industry*, Bell.

G. D. H. COLE (1952), *A Short History of the British Working Class Movement 1789-1947*, Allen and Unwin.

P. COLQUNHUNN (1814), *A Treatise on the Wealth, Power and Resources of the British Empire*, London.

P. DEANE (1956), 'Contemporary Estimates of National Income in the First Half of the Nineteenth Century', *Economic History Review.*

H. D. DICKINSON (1939), *The Economics of Socialism*, Oxford University Press.

M. DOBB (1937), *Political Economy and Capitalism*, Routledge and Kegan Paul.

E. DURKHEIM (1933), *The Division of Labour in Society*, Macmillan.

F. Y. EDGEWORTH (1877), *New and Old Methods of Ethics*, London.

W. A. ELTIS (1973), *Growth and Distribution*, Macmillan.

C. E. FERGUSON (1969), *The Neoclassical Theory of Production and Distribution*, Cambridge University Press.

B. FINE and L. HARRIS (1979), *Rereading* Capital, Macmillan.

A. L. FRIEDMAN (1977), *Industry and Labour*, Macmillan.

M. FRIEDMAN (1972), *Capitalism and Freedom*, Chicago University Press.

E. FROMM (1965), *The Sane Society*, Premier Books.

J. K. GALBRAITH (1952), *American Capitalism: The Concept of Countervailing Power*, Hamish Hamilton.

J. K. GALBRAITH (1958), *The Affluent Society*, Hamish Hamilton.

J. K. GALBRAITH (1967), *The New Industrial State*, Hamish Hamilton.

J. K. GALBRAITH (1974), *Economics and the Public Purpose*, Andre Deutsch.

L. GALLAWAY (1964), 'The Theory of Relative Shares', *Quarterly Journal of Economics*.

A. GLYN and B. SUTCLIFFE (1972), *British Capitalism, Workers and the Profits Squeeze*, Penguin.

J. A. C. GOBINEAU (1855), *Essay on the Inequality of the Human Races*, Paris.

J. de V. GRAAFF (1957), *Theoretical Welfare Economics*, Cambridge University Press.

J. GRAY (1825), *A Lecture on Human Happiness*, London.

R. HEILBRONER (1960), *The Future as History*, Harper and Row.

A. HELLER (1974), *The Theory of Need in Marx*, Allison and Busby.

J. A. HOBSON (1900), *The Economics of Distribution*, Macmillan.

T. HODGSKIN (1825), *Labour Defended Against the Claims of Capital*, London.

S. HOLLAND (1975), *The Socialist Challenge*, Quartet.

B. HORVAT (1968), *Toward a Theory of Planned Economy*, Yugoslav Institute for Economic Research.

M. C. HOWARD and J. E. KING (1975), *The Political Economy of Marx*, Longman.

S. HYMER and F. ROOSEVELT (1972), Comment on 'The Political Economy of the New Left', *Quarterly Journal of Economics*.

W. S. JEVONS (1871), *The Theory of Political Economy*, Macmillan.

H. G. JOHNSON (1973), *The Theory of Income Distribution*, Gray-Mills.

N. KALDOR (1956), 'Alternative Theories of Distribution', *Review of Economic Studies*.

J. M. KEYNES (1936), *The General Theory of Employment, Interest and Money*, Macmillan.

F. H. KNIGHT (1921), *Risk, Uncertainty and Profit*, Houghton Mifflin.

O. LANGE (1935),. 'Marxian Economics and Modern Economic Theory', *Review of Economic Studies*.

A. P. LERNER (1939), 'From Vulgar Political Economy to Vulgar Marxism', *Journal of Political Economy*.

A. P. LERNER (1972), 'A Note on "Understanding the Marxian Notion of Exploitation,"' *Journal of Economic Literature*.

W. A. LEWIS (1949), *The Principles of Economic Planning*, Dennis Dobson.

A. LINDBECK (1977), *The Political Economy of the New Left*, Harper and Row.

R. G. LIPSEY and K. LANCASTER (1956-7), 'The General Theory of Second Best', *Review of Economic Studies*.

D. LOCKWOOD and J. H. GOLDTHORPE (1968), *The Affluent Worker*, Cambridge University Press.

M. LONGFIELD (1833), *Lectures on Political Economy, Delivered in Trinity and Michaelmas Terms*, Dublin.

T. R. MALTHUS (1798), *An Essay on the Principle of Population*, London.

J. MARCHAL (1957), 'Wage Theory and Social Groups', in *The Theory of Wage Determination*, edited by J. T. Dunlop, Macmillan.

A. MARSHALL (1890), *Principles of Economics*, Macmillan.

F. MATTHEWS (1971), 'The Building Guilds', in *Essays in Labour History 1886-1923*, edited by A. Briggs and J. Saville, Macmillan.

J. S. MILL (1848), *Principles of Political Economy*, Longmans (1909).

E. NELL (1967), 'Theories of Growth and Theories of Value', *Economic Development and Cultural Change*.

D. M. NUTI (1970), '"Vulgar Economy" in the Theory of Distibution', *De Economist*.

S. OLIVIER (1888), *Capital and Land*, Fabian Tract No. 7.

L. L. PASINETTI (1962), 'Rate of Profit and Income Distribution in Relation to the Rate of Economic Growth', *Review of Economic Studies*.

S. N. PATTEN (1907), *The New Basis of Civilisation*, Macmillan.

A. C. PIGOU (1920), *The Economics of Welfare*, Macmillan.

K. POPPER (1945), *The Open Society and Its Enemies*, Routledge and Kegan Paul.

P. RAVENSTONE (1821), *A Few Doubts as to the Correctness of Some Opinions Generally Entertained on the Subjects of Population and Political Economy*, London.

J. RAWLS (1972), *Theory of Justice*, Clarendon Press.

S. READ (1829), *Political Economy: An Inquiry into the Natural Grounds of Right to Vendible Property, or Wealth*, Edinburgh.

M. W. REDER (1959), 'Alternative Theories of Labour's Share', in *The Allocation of Economic Resources*, edited by M. Abramovitz, Stanford University Press.

D. RICARDO (1817), *On the Principles of Political Economy and Taxation*, London.

J. ROBINSON (1933), *The Economics of Imperfect Competition*, Macmillan.

J. ROBINSON (1942), *An Essay on Marxian Economics*, Macmillan.

J. ROBINSON (1961), 'Prelude to "A Critique of Economic Theory",' *Oxford Economic Papers*.

J. ROBINSON (1965), 'Piero Sraffa and the Rate of Exploitation', *New Left Review*.

B. S. ROWNTREE (1901), *Poverty: A Study of Town Life*, Macmillan.

P. A. SAMUELSON (1955), *Economics: An Introductory Analysis*, McGraw-Hill.

P. A. SAMUELSON (1962), 'Parable and Realism in Capital Theory: The Surrogate Production Function', *Review of Economic Studies.*

P. A. SAMUELSON (1971), 'Understanding the Marxian Notion of Exploitation: A Summary of the So-Called Transformation Problem between Marxian Values and Competitive Prices', *Journal of Economic Literature.*

P. SARGANT FLORENCE (1953), *The Logic of British and American Industry*, Routledge and Kegan Paul.

J. B. SAY (1803), *A Treatise on Political Economy*, Paris.

J. A. SCHUMPETER (1942), *Capitalism, Socialism and Democracy*, Allen and Unwin.

G. P. SCROPE (1833), *Principles of Political Economy: Deducted from the Natural Laws of Social Welfare, and Applied to the Present State of Britain*, London.

F. SETON (1957), 'The "Transformation Problem"', *Review of Economic Studies.*

J. R. SHACKLETON (1976), 'Is Workers' Self-Management the Answer?', *National Westminster Bank Quarterly Review.*

G. B. SHAW (1937), *The Intelligent Woman's Guide to Socialism, Capitalism, Sovietism and Fascism*, Penguin.

A. SMITH (1776), *An Enquiry into the Nature and Causes of the Wealth of Nations*, Edinburgh.

A. SOHN-RETHEL (1978), *Intellectual and Manual Labour*, Macmillan.

P. SRAFFA (1960), *Production of Commodities by Means of Commodities*, Cambridge University Press.

J. STRACHEY (1936), *The Theory and Practice of Socialism*, Gollancz.

J. STRACHEY (1956), *Contemporary Capitalism*, Gollancz.

P. M. SWEEZY (1946), *The Theory of Capitalist Development*, Dobson.

P. M. SWEEZY (1972), *Modern Capitalism*, Monthly Review Press.

A. J. TAYLOR (1960), 'Progress and Poverty in Britain, 1780-1850: A Re-Appraisal', *History.*

F. W. TAYLOR (1911), *Principles of Scientific Management*, Harper.

W. THOMPSON (1824), *An Inquiry into the Principles of the Distribution of Wealth*, London.

J. VANEK (1970), *The General Theory of Labour-Managed Market Economies*, Cornell University Press.

L. WALRAS (1954), *Elements of Pure Economics*, edited by W. Jaffa, Allen and Unwin.

J. WESTERGAARD and H. RESLER (1975), *Class in a Capitalist Society*, Heinemann.

P. H. WICKSTEED (1894), *An Essay on the Coordination of the Laws of Distribution*, London.

Name Index

Subject Index